Cross Stitch
TEDDIES

Cross Stitch
TEDDIES

Over 200 teddy-themed charts for cross stitch

Kandour Ltd

Published by
Kandour Ltd
1-3 Colebrooke Place
London N1 8HZ
UNITED KINGDOM

This edition printed in 2006
for Bookmart Ltd
Registered Number 2372865
Trading as Bookmart Ltd
Blaby Road
Wigston
Leicester LE18 4SE

First published 2006

10 9 8 7 6 5 4 3 2 1

Author: Sue Whiting
Design and art direction: Cutting Edge Media
Production: Karen Lomax

Printed and bound in China
ISBN 1-904756-57-3

Contents

Ballet Bears

Put on that tutu and start stitching a card that is guaranteed to delight any budding ballerina! And there's no need to limit these charming designs to just greeting cards – why not embroider one on your favourite little girl's dancing kit bag too? Or frame one or two as pictures for her bedroom

BALLET BEARS KEY

★ **Cross stitch in two strands**

	DMC	Anchor	Madeira	
·	B5200	1	2401	white
◤	210	108	0802	lilac
∽	211	342	0801	light lilac
*	352	9	0303	salmon
∩	353	6	2605	light salmon
★	415	398	1802	grey
\	676	891	2208	light tan
◲	680	901	2210	dark tan
$	729	890	2209	tan
×	762	234	1804	light grey
◆	893	33	0413	dark pink
♡	894	31	0414	pink
✪	907	255	1308	green
⋄	973	290	0105	yellow
■	3021	905	1904	brown

★ **Backstitch in one strand**

——	3021	905	1904	brown

★ **STITCH COUNT** 60 high x 40 wide

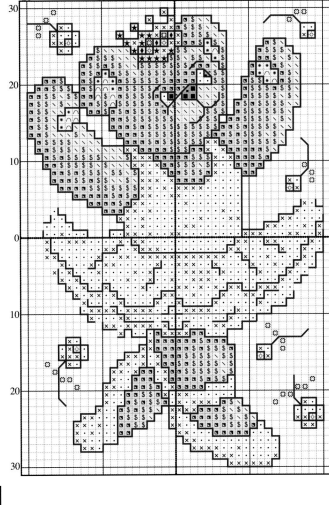

Above: **Pierina**
Shown bottom left in the photograph, this little bear is dressed all in white.

Left: **Moira**
This modest little bear likes to keep her knees covered with her longer dress.

Top left: *The key for all six ballerina charts – the two shown here and the four shown overleaf.*

Worked on a 14 count fabric, each ballet bear measures about 11 cm (4½ ins) tall and 7 cm (2¾ ins) wide when completed.

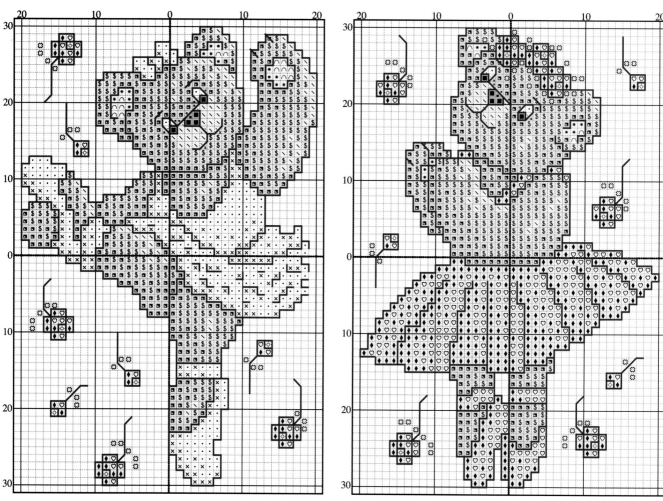

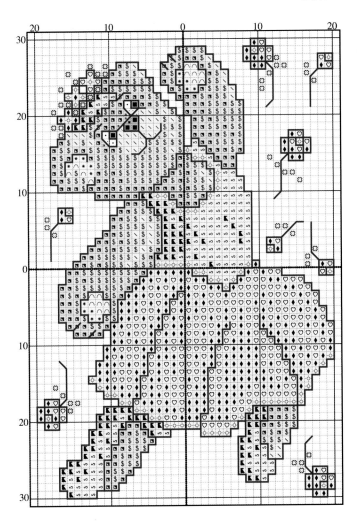

Left: **Anna**
Shown top left in the photograph, this lively little bear is dressed in shades of pink and lilac.

Opposite left: **Alicia**
Shown far right in the photograph, this energetic little bear likes to show off her skills.

Opposite right: **Darcey**
Shown bottom right in the photograph, this demure little bear is thanking her audience.

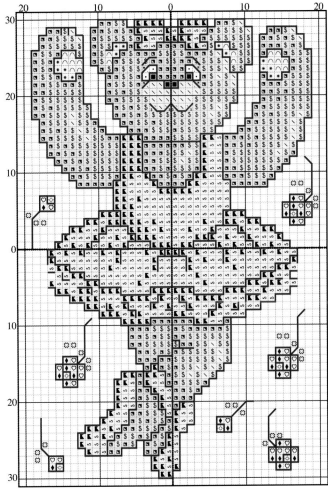

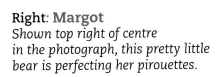

Right: **Margot**
Shown top right of centre in the photograph, this pretty little bear is perfecting her pirouettes.

Cute & Cuddly

Create a greeting card for every occasion featuring these cute and cuddly little teddies. Each design features a sweet little teddy dressed to impress – and each would make the perfect accompaniment to a gift of a real teddy!

Each teddy design is about 5 cm (2 ins) wide and just under 7.5 cm (3 ins) tall when worked on a 14 count fabric. Choose toning card mounts, as shown here, or make a real impact by using a strong contrasting colour. Try varying the colour of the clothes the teddies are wearing to match in with the gift you are giving, or simply to refect their favourite colour. Our teddies are all worked as greeting cards - but why not use them to decorate other items? Sprinkle a few teddies over a baby blanket, or place just one inside a trinket box lid, or paperweight.

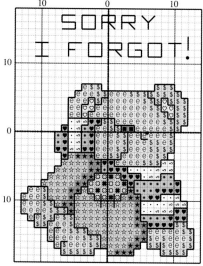

Left: *The chart for this design is shown below, and the key is given opposite.*

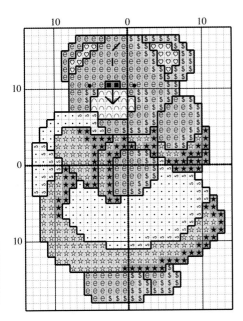

Right: *The chart for this design is given above, and the key is shown below.*

BEAR IN APRON KEY

★ Cross stitch in two strands

	DMC	Anchor	Madeira	
·	blanc	2	2402	white
■	310	403	2400	black
$	436	1045	2011	tan
⌒	712	926	2101	cream
e	738	367	2013	light tan
∽	762	234	1804	light grey
★	798	137	0912	blue
☆	799	145	0910	light blue
♡	3326	36	0606	pink

★ Backstitch in one strand

	DMC	Anchor	Madeira	
——	310	403	2400	black

★ French knots in one strand

	DMC	Anchor	Madeira	
●	310	403	2400	black

★ STITCH COUNT 35 high x 26 wide

SORRY I FORGOT KEY

★ Cross stitch in two strands

	DMC	Anchor	Madeira	
·	blanc	2	2402	white
■	310	403	2400	black
$	436	1045	2011	tan
*	606	334	0209	bright red
e	738	367	2013	light tan
∽	762	234	1804	light grey
★	798	137	0912	blue
☆	799	145	0910	light blue
♥	817	13	0210	dark red
✖	911	205	1214	green
✿	954	203	1207	light green
♡	3326	36	0606	pink

★ Backstitch in one strand

	DMC	Anchor	Madeira	
——	310	403	2400	black

★ French knots in one strand

	DMC	Anchor	Madeira	
●	310	403	2400	black

★ STITCH COUNT 35 high x 26 wide

HUG ME LOTS KEY

★ **Cross stitch in two strands**

	DMC	Anchor	Madeira	
■	310	403	2400	black
◨	434	310	2009	brown
$	436	1045	2011	tan
∩	712	926	2101	cream
e	738	367	2013	light tan
★	798	137	0912	blue
☆	799	145	0910	light blue
♡	3326	36	0606	pink

★ **Backstitch in one strand**

——	310	403	2400	black

★ **French knots in one strand**

●	310	403	2400	black

★ **STITCH COUNT** 35 high x 30 wide

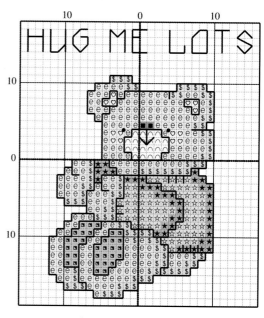

SCHOOL BOY BEAR KEY

★ Cross stitch in two strands

	DMC	Anchor	Madeira	
·	blanc	2	2402	white
■	310	403	2400	black
♥	350	11	0213	red
◨	434	310	2009	brown
$	436	1045	2011	tan
∩	712	926	2101	cream
⟡	727	293	0110	light yellow
e	738	367	2013	light tan
★	798	137	0912	blue
☆	799	145	0910	light blue
♡	3326	36	0606	pink

★ Backstitch in one strand

——	310	403	2400	black

★ French knots in one strand

●	310	403	2400	black

★ STITCH COUNT 31 high x 28 wide

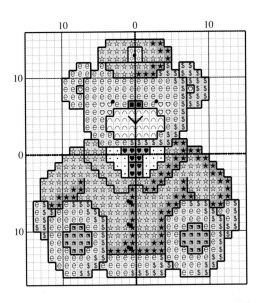

BEAR IN PURPLE DRESS KEY

★ **Cross stitch in two strands**

	DMC	Anchor	Madeira	
·	blanc	2	2402	white
■	310	403	2400	black
t	340	118	0902	light purple
◣	434	310	2009	brown
$	436	1045	2011	tan
∩	712	926	2101	cream
⋄	727	293	0110	light yellow
e	738	367	2013	light tan
♡	3326	36	0606	pink
♭	3746	1030	2702	purple

★ **Backstitch in one strand**

——	310	403	2400	black

★ **French knots in one strand**

●	310	403	2400	black

★ **STITCH COUNT** 34 high x 28 wide

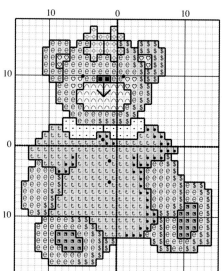

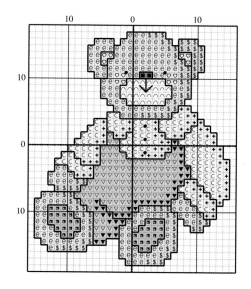

BEAR IN DUNGAREES KEY

★ **Cross stitch in two strands**

	DMC	Anchor	Madeira	
■	310	403	2400	black
◣	434	310	2009	brown
$	436	1045	2011	tan
+	444	291	0106	yellow
C	445	288	0103	light yellow
▼	701	227	1305	green
▽	703	238	1307	light green
∩	712	926	2101	cream
e	738	367	2013	light tan
♡	3326	36	0606	pink

★ **Backstitch in one strand**

——	310	403	2400	black

★ **French knots in one strand**

●	310	403	2400	black

★ **STITCH COUNT** 35 high x 30 wide

BEAR IN RED DRESS KEY

★ Cross stitch in two strands

	DMC	Anchor	Madeira	
·	blanc	2	2402	white
◊	210	108	0802	lilac
■	310	403	2400	black
◩	434	310	2009	brown
$	436	1045	2011	tan
*	606	334	0209	bright red
∩	712	926	2101	cream
e	738	367	2013	light tan
∽	762	234	1804	light grey
♥	817	13	0210	dark red
♡	3326	36	0606	pink

★ Backstitch in one strand

——	310	403	2400	black

★ French knots in one strand

●	310	403	2400	black

★ STITCH COUNT 30 high x 28 wide

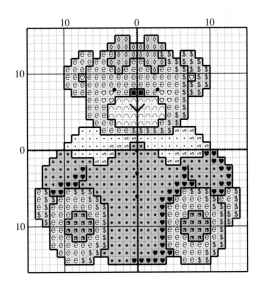

Summertime Ted

Surrounded by summer flowers, the teddy in this stunning framed picture is definitely sitting pretty on a patchwork quilt

The chart for this stunning framed picture design is shown above, and the key is given opposite.

Worked on a 14 count fabric, the completed design is just under 19 cm (7½ ins) square.

Our picture was framed without a mount board in a simple wood-effect frame. Why not make your picture into a really big eye-catching masterpiece by using a toning colour mount board and a bigger frame? Pick out colours from within the embroidery - try a soft green for the mount board and a deep pink for the frame. Or, if the picture is to hang in a boy's room, pick out the blue and green tones.

SUMMER TEDDY KEY

★ **Cross stitch in two strands**

	DMC	Anchor	Madeira	
๑	164	240	1209	soft green
■	310	403	2400	black
I	676	891	2208	sand
◊	704	237	1308	bright green
☆	728	305	0107	yellow
·φ·	729	890	2209	dark sand
v	772	259	1604	light green
▼	780	309	2212	dark tan
✿	905	257	1412	green
♭	913	204	1212	mint green
♡	963	73	0502	light pink
t	964	185	1112	turquoise
○	977	1002	2302	rust
♥	986	246	1404	dark green
⚲	3326	36	0606	pink
☾	3607	87	0708	cerise
C	3823	386	2512	cream
⬈	3829	901	2210	tan
♥	3832	1024	0604	very dark pink
◼	3833	1023	0609	dark pink

★ **Backstitch in one strand**

	DMC	Anchor	Madeira	
——	150	59	0508	cherry red
——	310	403	2400	black
——	898	380	2006	dark brown
——	986	246	1404	dark green

★ **STITCH COUNT** 98 high x 98 wide

Happy Father's Day!

*Stitch a card for dad using one of these jolly designs. Just pick
out dad's favourite sport and get stitching. You could even match the
bear's sports kit to the colours of dad's favourite team!*

TENNIS TED KEY

★ **Cross stitch in two strands**

	DMC	Anchor	Madeira	
·	blanc	2	2402	white
■	310	403	2400	black
∩	415	398	1802	grey
℮	435	1046	2010	brown
$	436	1045	2011	light brown
▽	518	1039	1106	blue
t	676	891	2208	sand
e	729	890	2209	dark sand
☾	907	255	1308	green

★ **Backstitch in one strand**

| ——— | 3799 | 236 | 1713 | dark grey |

★ **STITCH COUNT** 40 high x 40 wide

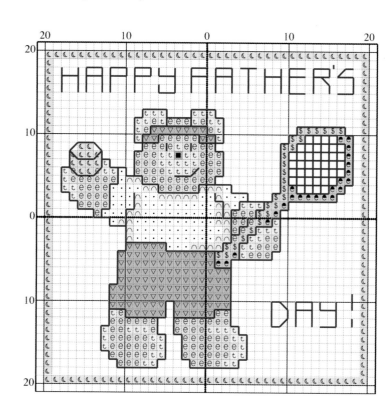

FISHING TED KEY

★ **Cross stitch in two strands**

	DMC	Anchor	Madeira	
☆	209	109	0803	lilac
■	310	403	2400	black
♡	349	13	0212	red
∩	415	398	1802	grey
t	676	891	2208	sand
e	729	890	2209	dark sand
·◇·	743	302	0113	yellow
\	744	301	0112	light yellow
☾	907	255	1308	green

★ **Backstitch in one strand**

| ——— | 3799 | 236 | 1713 | dark grey |

★ **STITCH COUNT** 40 high x 40 wide

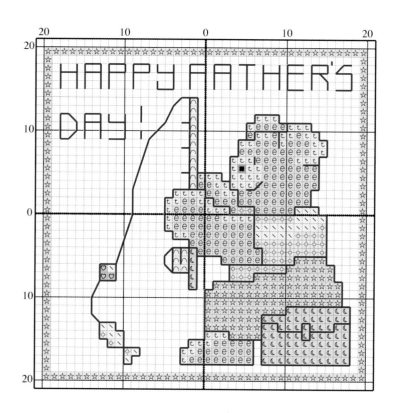

KARATE TED KEY

★ **Cross stitch in two strands**

	DMC	Anchor	Madeira	
·	blanc	2	2402	white
■	310	403	2400	black
■	349	13	0212	red
∩	415	398	1802	grey
▽	518	1039	1106	blue
t	676	891	2208	sand
e	729	890	2209	dark sand

★ **Backstitch in one strand**

	DMC	Anchor	Madeira	
———	3799	236	1713	dark grey

★ **STITCH COUNT** 40 high x 40 wide

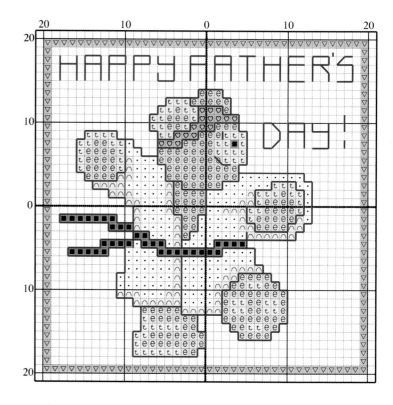

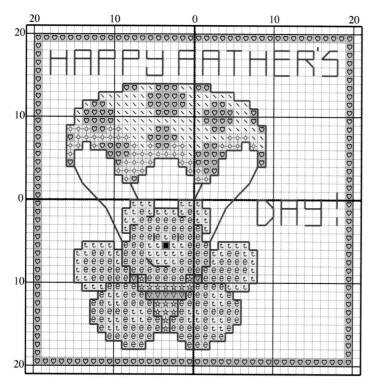

PARACHUTING TED KEY

★ **Cross stitch in two strands**

	DMC	Anchor	Madeira	
☆	209	109	0803	lilac
■	310	403	2400	black
♡	349	13	0212	red
▽	518	1039	1106	blue
t	676	891	2208	sand
e	729	890	2209	dark sand
⋄	743	302	0113	yellow
\	744	301	0112	light yellow

★ **Backstitch in one strand**

	DMC	Anchor	Madeira	
———	3799	236	1713	dark grey

★ **STITCH COUNT** 40 high x 40 wide

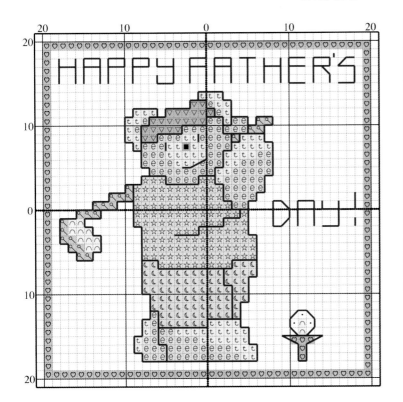

SKIING TED KEY

★ Cross stitch in two strands

	DMC	Anchor	Madeira	
·	blanc	2	2402	white
☆	209	109	0803	lilac
■	310	403	2400	black
▽	518	1039	1106	blue
t	676	891	2208	sand
e	729	890	2209	dark sand
⋄	743	302	0113	yellow
⟍	744	301	0112	light yellow

★ Backstitch in one strand

——	3799	236	1713	dark grey

★ **STITCH COUNT** 40 high x 40 wide

FOOTBALL TED KEY

★ Cross stitch in two strands

	DMC	Anchor	Madeira	
·	blanc	2	2402	white
■	310	403	2400	black
♡	349	13	0212	red
∩	415	398	1802	grey
t	676	891	2208	sand
e	729	890	2209	dark sand
⋄	743	302	0113	yellow
⟍	744	301	0112	light yellow

★ Backstitch in one strand

——	3799	236	1713	dark grey

★ **STITCH COUNT** 40 high x 40 wide

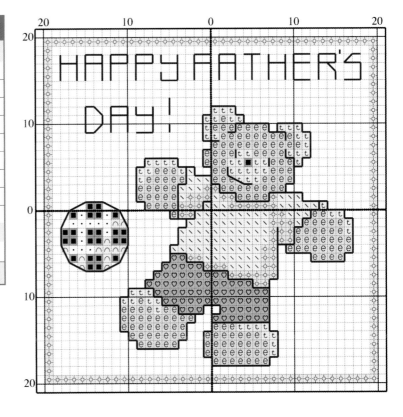

GOLFING TED KEY

★ **Cross stitch in two strands**

	DMC	Anchor	Madeira	
·	blanc	2	2402	white
☆	209	109	0803	lilac
■	310	403	2400	black
♡	349	13	0212	red
⚲	414	235	1714	grey
∩	415	398	1802	light grey
▽	518	1039	1106	blue
t	676	891	2208	sand
e	729	890	2209	dark sand
☾	907	255	1308	green

★ **Backstitch in one strand**

——	3799	236	1713	dark grey

★ **STITCH COUNT** 40 high x 40 wide

Each of these ten designs is about 7.5 cm (3 ins) square when worked on a 14 count fabric. Choose from golf, cricket, football, tennis, fishing, karate, skiing, parachuting, weight lifting and skate boarding.

And don't forget that they don't have to just be used on greeting cards - just leave out the message and use the "sporting heroes" to decorate his sports bag or towel. Or replace the greeting with "happy birthday" and they are ideal for any sportsman!

CRICKET TED KEY

★ **Cross stitch in two strands**

	DMC	Anchor	Madeira	
·	blanc	2	2402	white
■	310	403	2400	black
∩	415	398	1802	grey
℮	435	1046	2010	brown
$	436	1045	2011	light brown
t	676	891	2208	sand
e	729	890	2209	dark sand
☾	907	255	1308	green

★ **Backstitch in one strand**

——	3799	236	1713	dark grey

★ **STITCH COUNT** 40 high x 40 wide

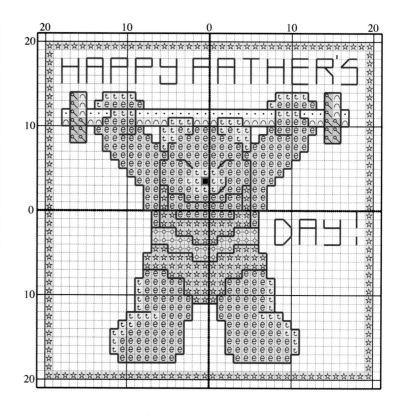

SNOW BOARDING TED KEY

★ Cross stitch in two strands

	DMC	Anchor	Madeira	
·	blanc	2	2402	white
■	310	403	2400	black
♡	349	13	0212	red
∩	415	398	1802	grey
▽	518	1039	1106	blue
t	676	891	2208	sand
e	729	890	2209	dark sand
-◇-	743	302	0113	yellow
╲	744	301	0112	light yellow

★ Backstitch in one strand

——	3799	236	1713	dark grey

★ STITCH COUNT 40 high x 40 wide

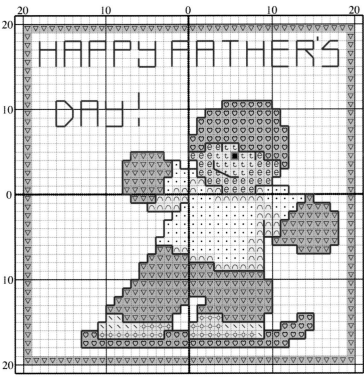

WEIGHT LIFTING TED KEY

★ Cross stitch in two strands

	DMC	Anchor	Madeira	
·	blanc	2	2402	white
☆	209	109	0803	lilac
■	310	403	2400	black
⚲	414	235	1714	grey
∩	415	398	1802	light grey
t	676	891	2208	sand
e	729	890	2209	dark sand
-◇-	743	302	0113	yellow

★ Backstitch in one strand

——	3799	236	1713	dark grey

★ STITCH COUNT 40 high x 40 wide

A Year of Bears!

Create your very own calendar of bears using these twelve charming pictures – each depicts a different month of the year.

Hang them all together to create a really big "calendar" or just hang one at a time, choosing just the right month for the time of year.

CALENDAR OF BEARS KEY

★ **Cross stitch in two strands**

	DMC	Anchor	Madeira	
·	blanc	2	2402	white
★	208	111	0804	lilac
☆	209	109	0803	light lilac
-◌-	307	289	0104	yellow
■	310	403	2400	black
↖	318	399	1801	grey
↖	415	398	1802	light grey
↗	434	310	2009	brown
◓	436	1045	2011	light brown
◊	445	288	0103	light yellow
◪	606	334	0209	bright red
▼	701	227	1305	green
▽	703	238	1307	light green
$	722	323	0307	peach
e	738	367	2013	light tan
K	798	137	0912	dark blue
K	799	145	0910	blue
∽	800	144	0908	sky blue
☾	809	130	0909	light blue
♥	817	13	0210	dark red
◑	912	209	1213	mint green
◔	954	203	1207	light mint
♡	957	50	0504	pink
⊠	970	925	0205	orange
v	3064	883	2312	beige

★ **Backstitch in one strand**

——	310	403	2400	black
——	606	334	0209	bright red
——	703	238	1307	light green
——	798	137	0912	dark blue
——	809	130	0909	light blue
——	970	925	0205	orange

★ **French knots in one strand**

●	307	289	0104	yellow
●	310	403	2400	black

★ **STITCH COUNT** 47 high x 40 wide

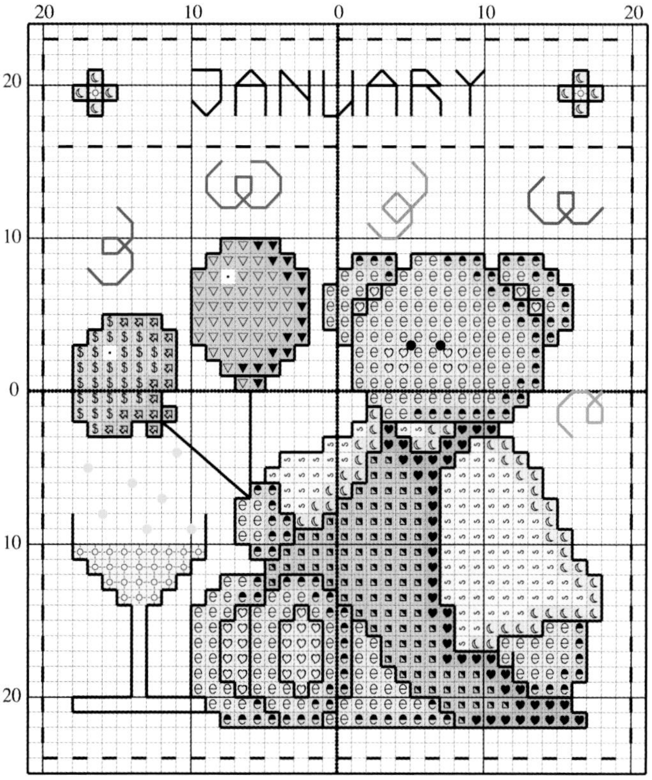

January *See in the new year with a party!*

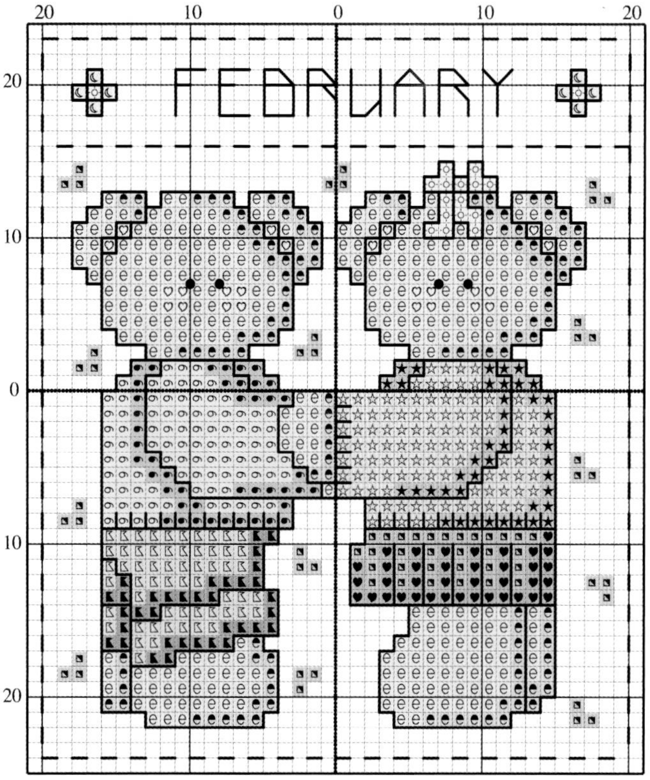

February *Be my Valentine!*

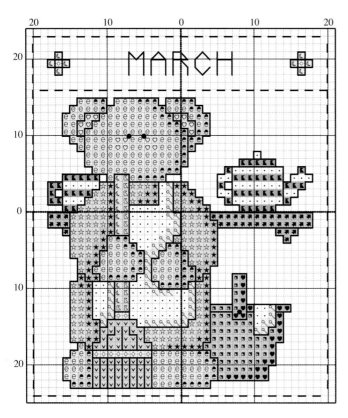

March *Mad march hares!*

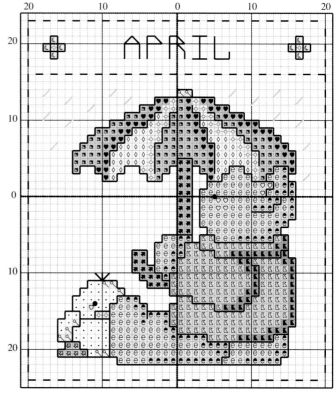

April *April showers*

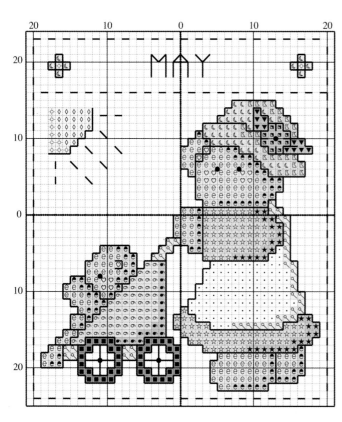

May *Summer's on it's way!*

CALENDAR OF BEARS KEY

★ Cross stitch in two strands

	DMC	Anchor	Madeira	
·	blanc	2	2402	white
★	208	111	0804	lilac
☆	209	109	0803	light lilac
-◇-	307	289	0104	yellow
■	310	403	2400	black
◤	318	399	1801	grey
◠	415	398	1802	light grey
◢	434	310	2009	brown
℮	436	1045	2011	light brown
◇	445	288	0103	light yellow
◘	606	334	0209	bright red
▼	701	227	1305	green
▽	703	238	1307	light green
$	722	323	0307	peach
℮	738	367	2013	light tan
◤	798	137	0912	dark blue
◪	799	145	0910	blue
﹏	800	144	0908	sky blue
☾	809	130	0909	light blue
♥	817	13	0210	dark red
●	912	209	1213	mint green
ை	954	203	1207	light mint
♡	957	50	0504	pink
⬈	970	925	0205	orange
⌄	3064	883	2312	beige

★ Backstitch in one strand

	DMC	Anchor	Madeira	
——	310	403	2400	black
——	606	334	0209	bright red
——	703	238	1307	light green
——	798	137	0912	dark blue
——	809	130	0909	light blue
——	970	925	0205	orange

★ French knots in one strand

	DMC	Anchor	Madeira	
●	307	289	0104	yellow
●	310	403	2400	black

★ STITCH COUNT 47 high x 40 wide

The key for all twelve charts.

June *Seaside fun*

CALENDAR OF BEARS KEY

	DMC	Anchor	Madeira	
★ Cross stitch in two strands				
·	blanc	2	2402	white
★	208	111	0804	lilac
☆	209	109	0803	light lilac
-○-	307	289	0104	yellow
■	310	403	2400	black
●	318	399	1801	grey
○	415	398	1802	light grey
◆	434	310	2009	brown
◐	436	1045	2011	light brown
◊	445	288	0103	light yellow
◘	606	334	0209	bright red
▼	701	227	1305	green
▽	703	238	1307	light green
$	722	323	0307	peach
e	738	367	2013	light tan
◣	798	137	0912	dark blue
◺	799	145	0910	blue
∽	800	144	0908	sky blue
☾	809	130	0909	light blue
♥	817	13	0210	dark red
◗	912	209	1213	mint green
○	954	203	1207	light mint
♡	957	50	0504	pink
☆	970	925	0205	orange
v	3064	883	2312	beige
★ Backstitch in one strand				
——	310	403	2400	black
——	606	334	0209	bright red
——	703	238	1307	light green
——	798	137	0912	dark blue
——	809	130	0909	light blue
——	970	925	0205	orange
★ French knots in one strand				
●	307	289	0104	yellow
●	310	403	2400	black
★ STITCH COUNT 47 high x 40 wide				

The key for all twelve charts.

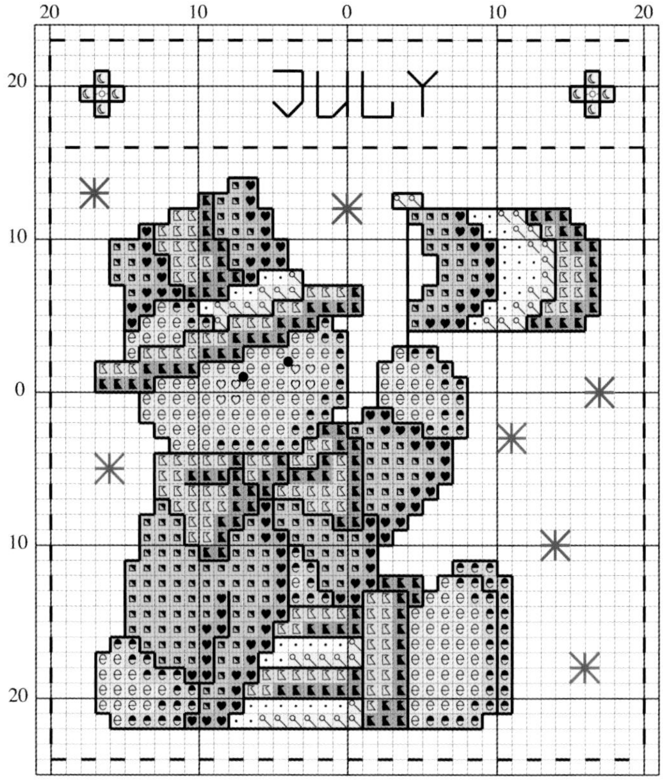

July *Independence Day*

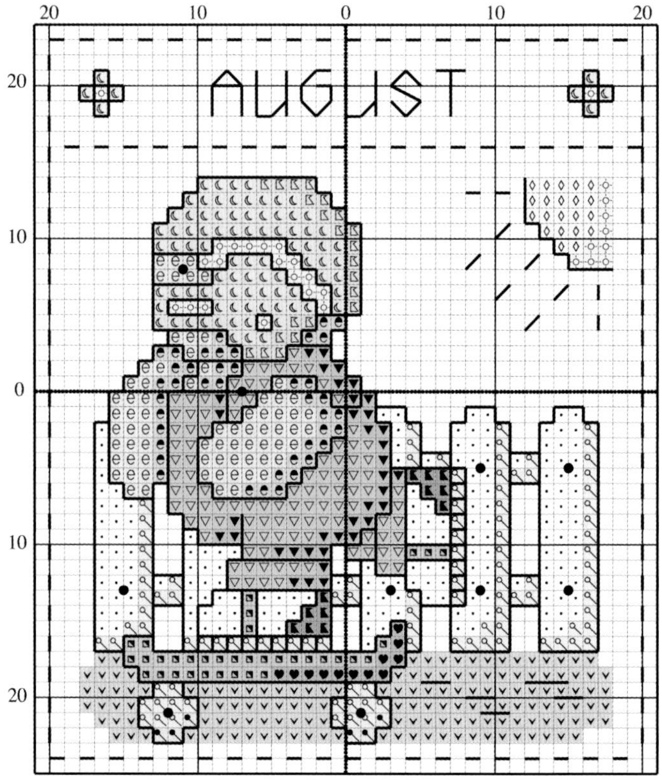

August *Summer fun*

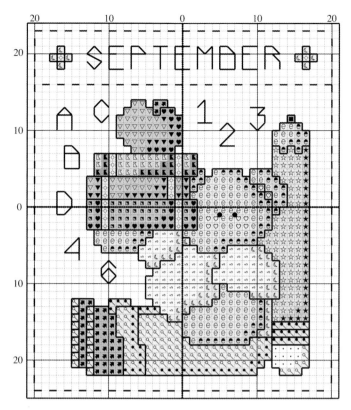

September *Back to school*

October *Happy halloween!*

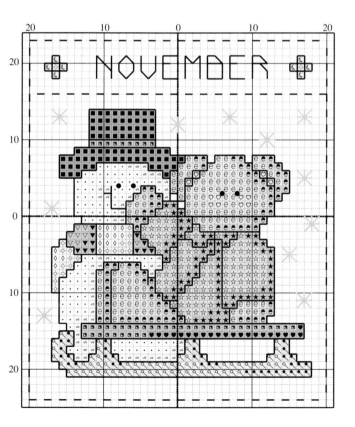

November *Fun in the snow*

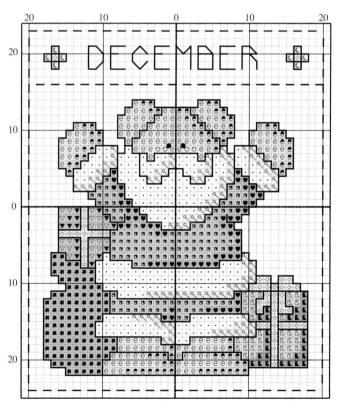

December *It's christmas!*

Musical Additons

Use these clever musical bears to add a note of individuality to your work. Use them to create personalised greeting cards, or as tiny framed pictures – you're bound to keep in tune!

Each of these twenty little charts features a musical bear and, when worked on a 14 count fabric, each design is just over 5 cm (2 ins) tall.

The key, shown left, gives the colour used for the number as shown on the chart – but you could easily alter this to a colour that matches in with what you are going to use the embroidery for.

MUSICAL TEDS KEY

★ Cross stitch in two strands

	DMG	Anchor	Madeira	
e	209	109	0803	lilac
■	310	403	2400	black
○	353	6	2605	peach
◤	553	98	0712	mauve
♡	666	46	0510	red
$	680	901	2210	dark gold
▼	702	226	1306	green
я	704	237	1308	light green
–	712	926	2101	cream
⋅φ⋅	725	305	0108	dark yellow
∩	726	295	0109	yellow
＼	727	293	0110	light yellow
⌣	729	890	2209	gold
☆	738	367	2013	tan
☽	739	366	2014	light tan
◪	3828	373	2103	hazlenut
✖	3839	175	0902	blue
♦	3852	306	2514	mustard

★ Backstitch in one strand

——	844	1041	1911	dark brown

★ MAXIMUM STITCH COUNT
30 high x 30 wide

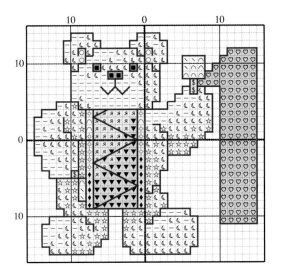

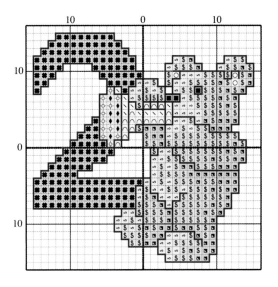

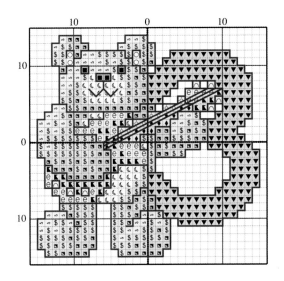

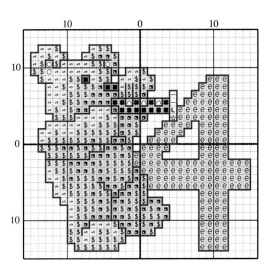

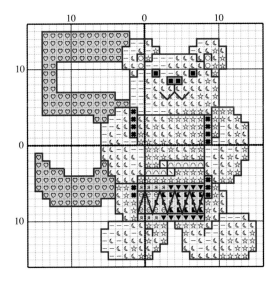

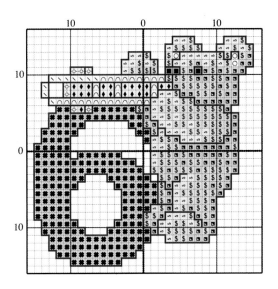

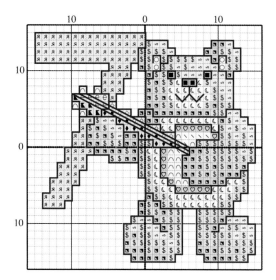

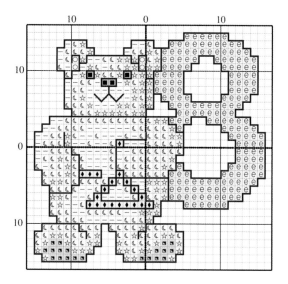

The key for all these charts is shown on the previous page.

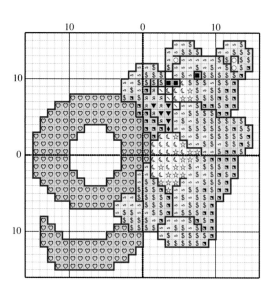

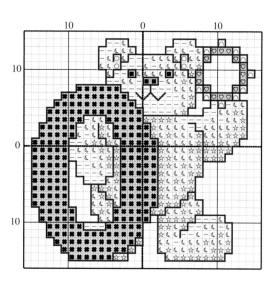

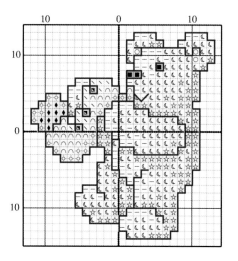

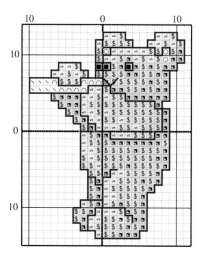

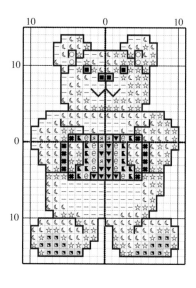

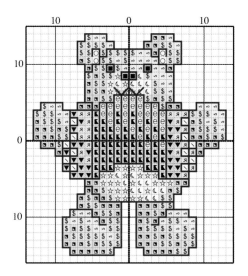

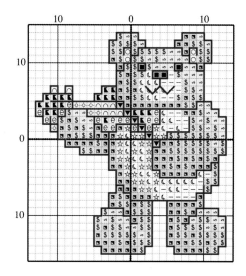

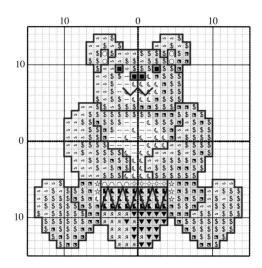

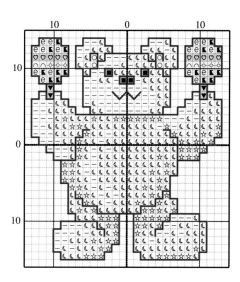

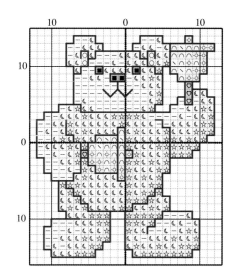

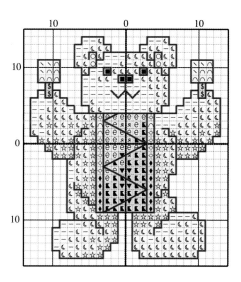

Busy Bears!

Make this clever sampler-style picture full of busy bears –
or use each of the individual elements to create little pictures.
The chart for the whole picture is given overleaf and there
are lots more little charts to use as well. More
than enough to keep you busy too!

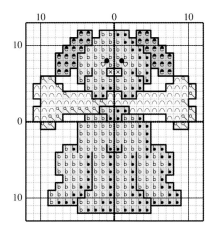

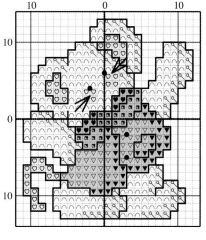

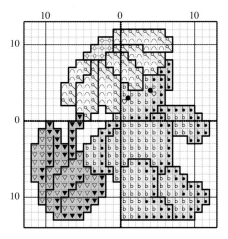

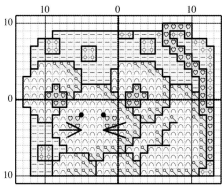

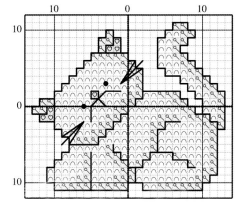

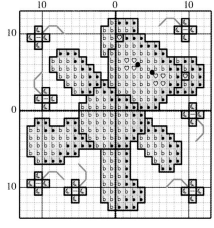

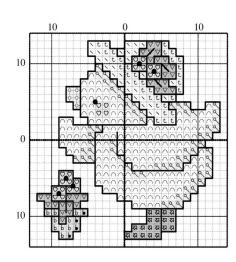

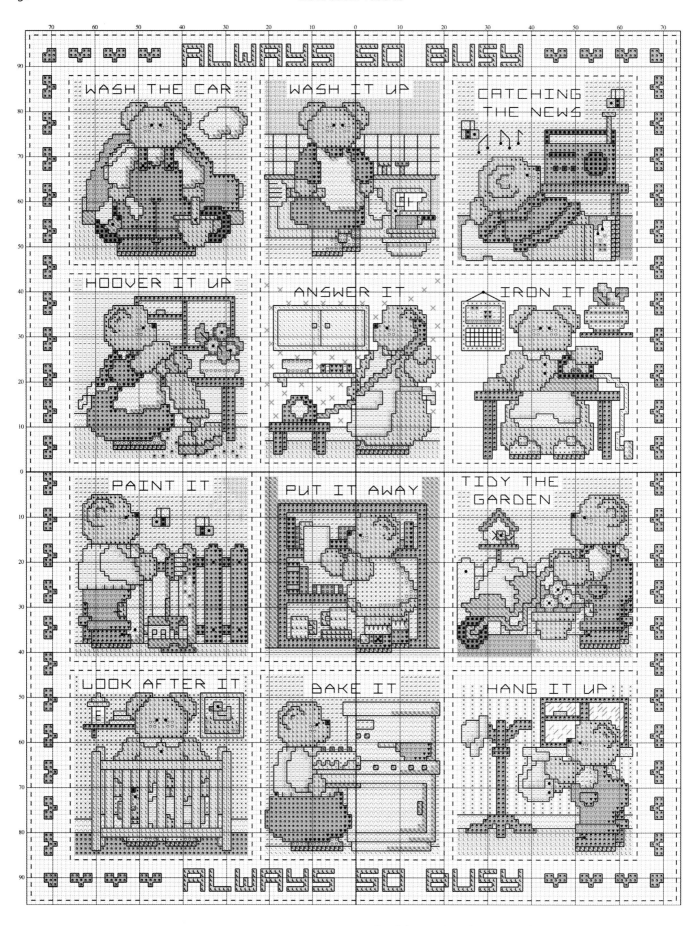

Above: *The chart for the sampler-style picture. Worked on a 14 count fabric, the completed picture is about 34 cm (13½ ins) tall and 28 cm (11 ins) wide. Why not use each of the twelve elements of this picture to make little pictures?*

ALWAYS SO BUSY KEY

★ **Cross stitch in two strands**

	DMC	Anchor	Madeira	
∩	blanc	2	2402	white
⋄	307	289	0104	bright yellow
■	310	403	2400	black
⚲	415	398	1802	grey
℮	434	310	2009	brown
♭	436	1045	2011	tan
◨	606	334	0209	bright red
▼	701	227	1305	green
▽	703	238	1307	light green
—	727	293	0110	yellow
♭	738	367	2013	light tan
☾	799	145	0910	dark blue
∽	800	144	0908	light blue
☾	809	130	0909	blue
♥	817	13	0210	dark red
×	818	23	0502	light pink
♡	957	50	0504	pink
⅃	970	925	0205	orange
\	3823	386	2512	light yellow
t	3855	311	2513	apricot

★ **Backstitch in one strand**

	DMC	Anchor	Madeira	
——	307	289	0104	bright yellow
——	310	403	2400	black
——	701	227	1305	green
——	799	145	0910	dark blue
——	970	925	0205	orange

★ **French knots in one strand**

	DMC	Anchor	Madeira	
●	310	403	2400	black

★ **STITCH COUNT** 192 high x 148 wide

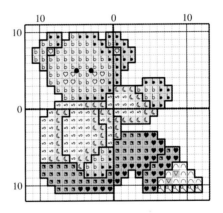

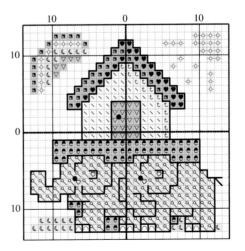

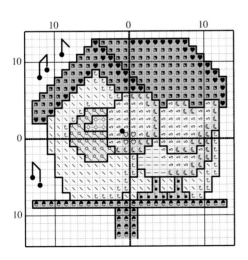

Use the little panels of the whole picture, shown right, to make individual tiny framed pictures like these shown here, left and below right!

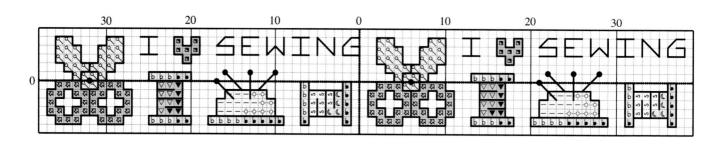

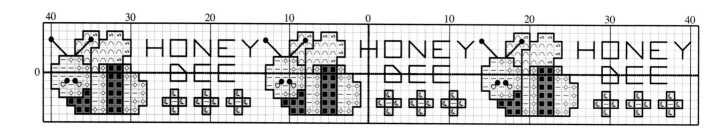

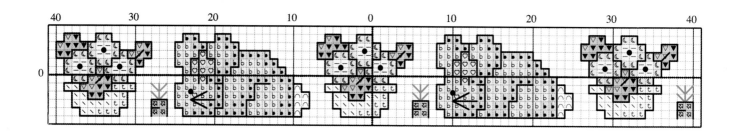

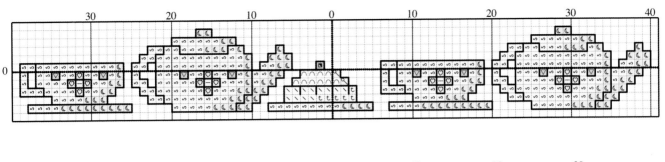

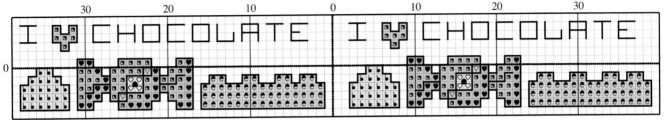

ALWAYS SO BUSY KEY

★ **Cross stitch in two strands**

	DMC	Anchor	Madeira	
∩	blanc	2	2402	white
⋄	307	289	0104	bright yellow
■	310	403	2400	black
⚲	415	398	1802	grey
℮	434	310	2009	brown
♭	436	1045	2011	tan
◨	606	334	0209	bright red
▼	701	227	1305	green
▽	703	238	1307	light green
−	727	293	0110	yellow
♭	738	367	2013	light tan
☾	799	145	0910	dark blue
∽	800	144	0908	light blue
☾	809	130	0909	blue
♥	817	13	0210	dark red
×	818	23	0502	light pink
♡	957	50	0504	pink
⚡	970	925	0205	orange
＼	3823	386	2512	light yellow
t	3855	311	2513	apricot
★ **Backstitch in one strand**				
——	307	289	0104	bright yellow
——	310	403	2400	black
——	701	227	1305	green
——	799	145	0910	dark blue
——	970	925	0205	orange
★ **French knots in one strand**				
●	310	403	2400	black

★ **STITCH COUNT** 192 high x 148 wide

Toasty-warm Teddies

*Send warmth and love to those you care about
with these toasty-warm winter teddy greeting cards –
they are just as apt for christmas as they are for winter birthdays.
There are six to choose from and each one will show just
how much you care. You could even use them for a winter wedding!*

CHEERS BEARS KEY

★ **Cross stitch in two strands**

	DMC	Anchor	Madeira	
·	B5200	1	2401	white
♥	321	9046	0510	dark red
☆	435	1046	2010	brown
∩	436	1045	2011	light brown
ꝿ	666	46	0210	bright red
▼	702	226	1306	green
t	703	238	1307	light green
−	712	926	2101	cream
⋄	726	295	0109	yellow
＼	727	293	0110	light yellow
я	739	366	2014	dark cream
○	761	1021	0404	pink
z	762	274	1804	light grey
■	938	381	2005	dark brown

★ **Backstitch in one strand**

	DMC	Anchor	Madeira	
——	3799	401	1713	dark grey

★ **STITCH COUNT** 40 high x 60 wide

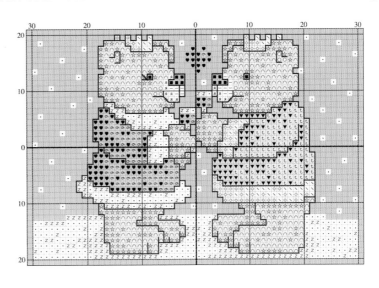

CUDDLING BEARS KEY

★ **Cross stitch in two strands**

	DMC	Anchor	Madeira	
·	B5200	1	2401	white
♥	321	9046	0510	dark red
◩	334	977	1004	dark blue
☆	435	1046	2010	brown
∩	436	1045	2011	light brown
ꝿ	666	46	0210	bright red
▼	702	226	1306	green
t	703	238	1307	light green
−	712	926	2101	cream
⋄	726	295	0109	yellow
＼	727	293	0110	light yellow
я	739	366	2014	dark cream
○	761	1021	0404	pink
z	762	274	1804	light grey
■	938	381	2005	dark brown
ᔓ	3755	140	0910	blue

★ **Backstitch in one strand**

	DMC	Anchor	Madeira	
——	3799	401	1713	dark grey

★ **STITCH COUNT** 40 high x 60 wide

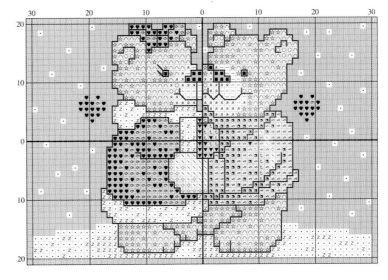

Worked on a 14 count fabric, each design is just over 10 cm (4 ins) by 7 cm (2½ ins).

HOLDING HANDS KEY

★ **Cross stitch in two strands**

	DMC	Anchor	Madeira	
·	B5200	1	2401	white
♥	321	9046	0510	dark red
◣	334	977	1004	dark blue
☆	435	1046	2010	brown
⌒	436	1045	2011	light brown
ග	666	46	0210	bright red
▼	702	226	1306	green
t	703	238	1307	light green
—	712	926	2101	cream
⬦	726	295	0109	yellow
＼	727	293	0110	light yellow
я	739	366	2014	dark cream
○	761	1021	0404	pink
z	762	274	1804	light grey
■	938	381	2005	dark brown
∽	3755	140	0910	blue

★ **Backstitch in one strand**

——	3799	401	1713	dark grey

★ **STITCH COUNT** 40 high x 60 wide

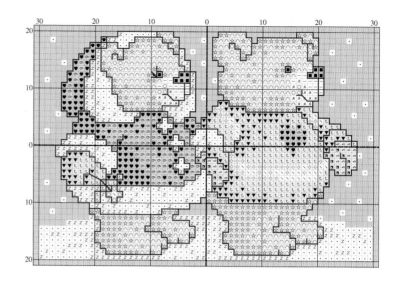

DANCING BEARS KEY

★ **Cross stitch in two strands**

	DMC	Anchor	Madeira	
·	B5200	1	2401	white
♥	321	9046	0510	dark red
◣	334	977	1004	dark blue
☆	435	1046	2010	brown
⌒	436	1045	2011	light brown
ග	666	46	0210	bright red
▼	702	226	1306	green
t	703	238	1307	light green
—	712	926	2101	cream
⬦	726	295	0109	yellow
＼	727	293	0110	light yellow
я	739	366	2014	dark cream
○	761	1021	0404	pink
z	762	274	1804	light grey
■	938	381	2005	dark brown
∽	3755	140	0910	blue

★ **Backstitch in one strand**

——	3799	401	1713	dark grey

★ **STITCH COUNT** 60 high x 40 wide

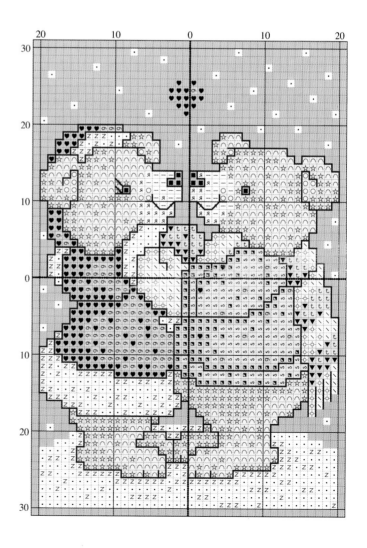

KISSING BEARS KEY

★ **Cross stitch in two strands**

	DMC	Anchor	Madeira	
·	B5200	1	2401	white
♥	321	9046	0510	dark red
◣	334	977	1004	dark blue
☆	435	1046	2010	brown
∩	436	1045	2011	light brown
၆	666	46	0210	bright red
▼	702	226	1306	green
t	703	238	1307	light green
—	712	926	2101	cream
-◇-	726	295	0109	yellow
＼	727	293	0110	light yellow
я	739	366	2014	dark cream
○	761	1021	0404	pink
z	762	274	1804	light grey
■	938	381	2005	dark brown
၁	3755	140	0910	blue

★ **Backstitch in one strand**

	DMC	Anchor	Madeira	
——	3799	401	1713	dark grey

★ **STITCH COUNT** 60 high x 40 wide

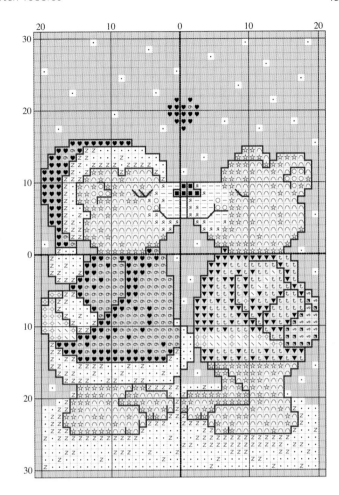

SKATING BEARS KEY

★ **Cross stitch in two strands**

	DMC	Anchor	Madeira	
·	B5200	1	2401	white
♥	321	9046	0510	dark red
◣	334	977	1004	dark blue
☆	435	1046	2010	brown
∩	436	1045	2011	light brown
၆	666	46	0210	bright red
▼	702	226	1306	green
t	703	238	1307	light green
—	712	926	2101	cream
-◇-	726	295	0109	yellow
＼	727	293	0110	light yellow
я	739	366	2014	dark cream
○	761	1021	0404	pink
z	762	274	1804	light grey
■	938	381	2005	dark brown
၁	3755	140	0910	blue

★ **Backstitch in one strand**

	DMC	Anchor	Madeira	
——	3799	401	1713	dark grey

★ **STITCH COUNT** 60 high x 40 wide

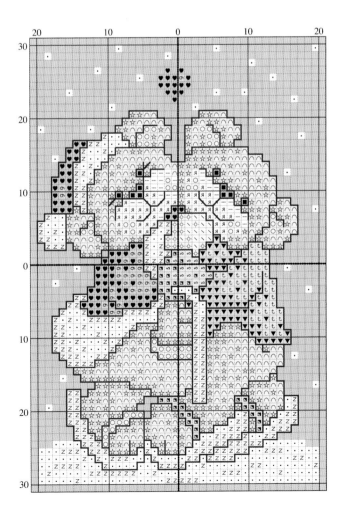

Bear Stockings

Make someone special one of these stunning christmas stockings to hang up on the mantel piece. Santa is bound to love them so much, he's bound to make sure they are filled with presents!

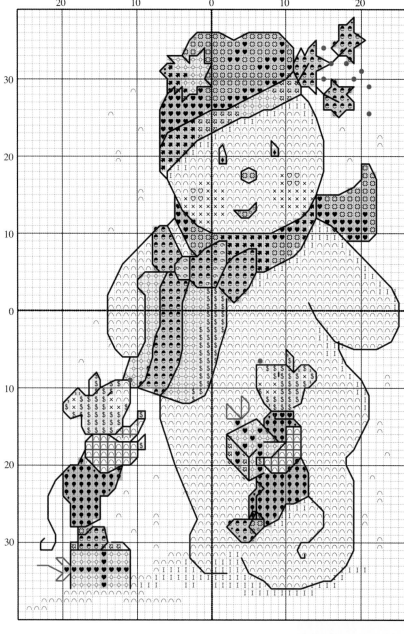

Snowman – *the chart is above.*

Teddy – *the chart is shown opposite.*

Santa – *the chart is shown on the previous page.*

The key for all 3 charts is given opposite.

STOCKINGS KEY

★ Cross stitch in two strands

	DMC	Anchor	Madeira	
∩	blanc	2	2402	white
■	310	403	2400	black
✿	350	11	0213	light red
Ϟ	676	891	2208	light sand
N	680	901	2210	dark sand
σ	703	238	1307	bright green
⌾	725	305	0108	yellow
$	729	890	2209	sand
⚐	740	316	0204	orange
⚵	742	303	0114	tangerine
♡	760	1022	0405	pink
▼	780	309	2212	tan
♥	798	137	0912	blue
♀	799	145	0910	light blue
♥	817	13	0210	red
·	819	271	0501	pink
℮	911	205	1214	green
I	3072	847	1805	grey
×	3713	1020	0502	light pink
◣	3799	236	1713	dark grey

★ Backstitch in one strand

	DMC	Anchor	Madeira	
——	310	403	2400	black
——	350	11	0213	light red
——	817	13	0210	red

★ French knots in one strand

	DMC	Anchor	Madeira	
●	310	403	2400	black
●	817	13	0210	red

★ MAXIMUM STITCH COUNT
82 high x 54 wide

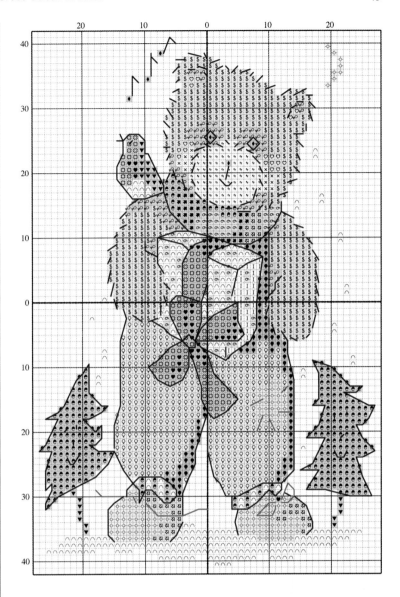

Worked on a 14 count fabric, each of these designs is about 15 cm (6 ins) tall and 10 cm (4 ins) wide.

To make the stockings shown in the photograph, the design was embroidered onto a piece of fabric that was then sewn onto a stocking. If you wish, you could embroider the design straight onto the stocking by using waste canvas.

These designs would make great framed pictures – or even really big and special christmas cards for a loved one.

Santa Ted

Make this masterpiece picture to create a family heirloom you'll be proud to bring out year after year

The picture here is framed within a simple wooden frame without a mount board, creating quite a neat and small picture to hang. But you could frame it with a wide mount board inside a much bigger frame to really make a statement on your wall. Try to keep the colour of the mount board quite light and subtle, choosing one of the paler shades within the embroidery, so that it does not detract from the design itself. The frame could be quite a wide frame in a strong colour - such as red - to create a bold outline to the work. This design would sit just as well in a modern frame as it would in a traditional one.

XMAS TED KEY

★ **Cross stitch in two strands**

	DMC	Anchor	Madeira	
·	B5200	1	2401	white
—	ecru	926	2404	ecru
▼	167	373	1607	dark brown
■	310	403	2400	black
e	312	979	1005	blue
v	350	11	0213	light red
♡	666	46	0210	red
♭	676	891	2208	sand
໑	702	226	1306	light green
♭	729	890	2209	dark sand
⚐	816	1005	0513	very dark red
♥	817	13	0210	dark red
◖	910	228	1302	green
∩	928	274	1709	grey
◪	3799	236	1713	dark grey
●	3818	923	2704	dark green
I	3823	386	2512	cream

★ **Cross stitch in two strands of metallic thread**

☼	5282			gold
☾	5289			purple
⚫	Art.273			black/gold

★ **Backstitch in one strand**

| ——— | 310 | 403 | 2400 | black |
| ——— | 801 | 359 | 2007 | dark brown |

★ **Backstitch in one strand of metallic thread**

| ——— | 5282 | | | gold |

★ **STITCH COUNT** 98 high x 95 wide

Make this cute Santa Ted to hang on your wall at christmas time. It's bound to become a firm family favourite that will come out year after year to delight the youngsters

Above: *The chart for the Santa Ted picture.*

Opposite: *The key for this chart.*

Worked on a 14 count fabric, the completed picture is just over 18 cm (7 ins) square.

Tumbling Teddies

Use this jolly alphabet to personalise your possessions – each and every letter has its own tumbling teddy. Embroideryyour intial for a pencil case, a notepad holder or a pencil pot and get the fun started!

Each teddy letter is about 6.5 cm (2½ ins) tall when worked on a 14 count fabric, but the width varies depending on which letter you work. The key for all these charts is shown opposite, top left, and here are the charts for letters A to H. Letters I to R are on the following two pages, and letters S to z follow those. You could vary the colour of the letter itself to match what you are using it for – but try to use the shades as given in the key for the bears so that they all match.

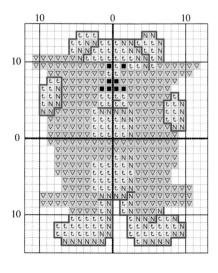

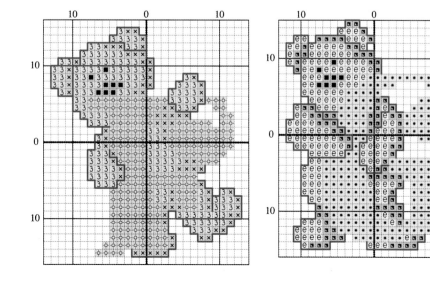

TUMBLING TEDS ABC KEY

★ Cross stitch in two strands

	DMC	Anchor	Madeira	
◊	209	109	0803	lilac
◣	301	1049	2306	tan
e	402	1047	2307	light tan
N	436	1045	2011	light brown
☆	518	1039	1106	sea blue
t	738	361	2913	dark cream
■	801	359	2007	dark brown
▽	912	209	1213	green
♥	956	41	0611	pink
✳	972	298	0107	yellow
⟡	3340	329	0301	apricot
◤	3839	176	2702	blue
×	3863	375	1912	dark beige
3	3864	388	1910	beige

★ Backstitch in one strand

——	801	359	2007	dark brown

★ MAXIMUM STITCH COUNT
33 high x 40 wide

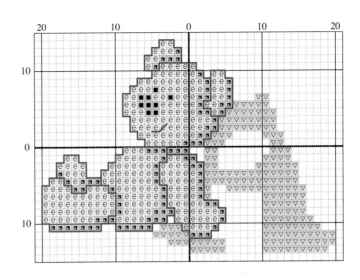

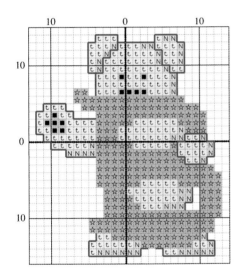

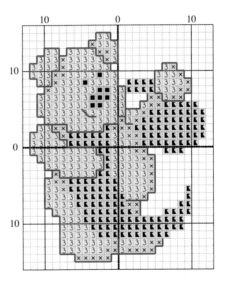

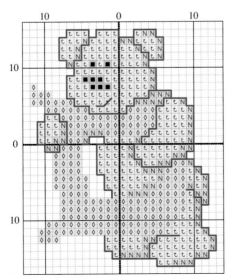

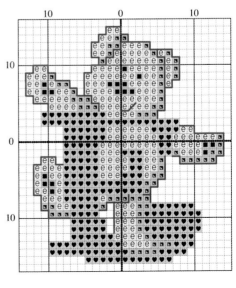

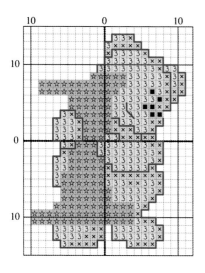

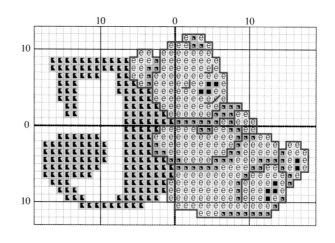

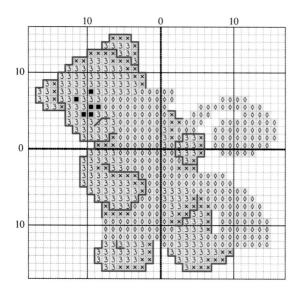

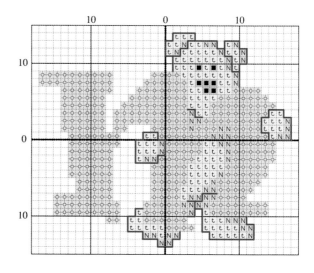

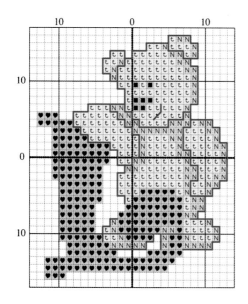

TUMBLING TEDS ABC KEY

★ **Cross stitch in two strands**

	DMC	Anchor	Madeira	
◊	209	109	0803	lilac
◣	301	1049	2306	tan
e	402	1047	2307	light tan
N	436	1045	2011	light brown
☆	518	1039	1106	sea blue
t	738	361	2913	dark cream
■	801	359	2007	dark brown
▽	912	209	1213	green
♥	956	41	0611	pink
*	972	298	0107	yellow
⋄	3340	329	0301	apricot
◤	3839	176	2702	blue
×	3863	375	1912	dark beige
3	3864	388	1910	beige

★ **Backstitch in one strand**

——	801	359	2007	dark brown

★ **MAXIMUM STITCH COUNT**
     33 high x 40 wide

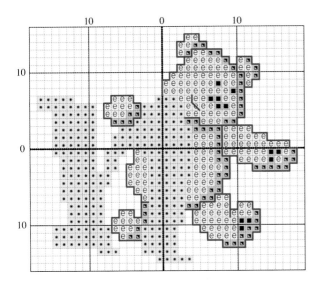

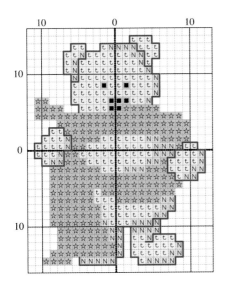

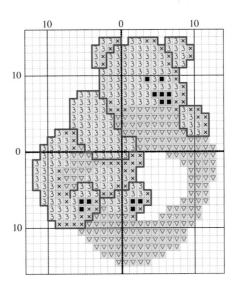

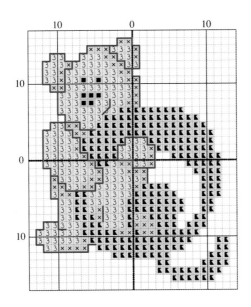

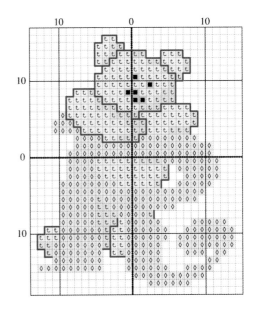

Use this jolly teddy alphabet to bring some fun to your desk! Or to brighten up the homework chore for your youngsters.

TUMBLING TEDS ABC KEY

★ **Cross stitch in two strands**

	DMC	Anchor	Madeira	
◊	209	109	0803	lilac
◣	301	1049	2306	tan
e	402	1047	2307	light tan
N	436	1045	2011	light brown
☆	518	1039	1106	sea blue
t	738	361	2913	dark cream
■	801	359	2007	dark brown
▽	912	209	1213	green
♥	956	41	0611	pink
✳	972	298	0107	yellow
⟡	3340	329	0301	apricot
◣	3839	176	2702	blue
×	3863	375	1912	dark beige
3	3864	388	1910	beige

★ **Backstitch in one strand**

——	801	359	2007	dark brown

★ **MAXIMUM STITCH COUNT**
33 high x 40 wide

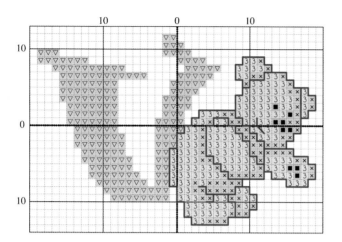

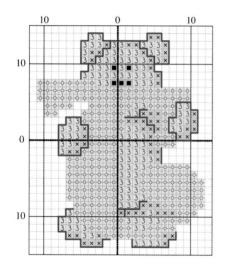

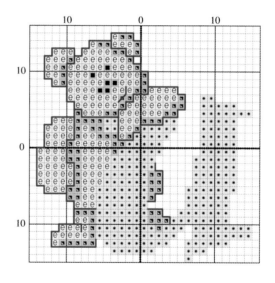

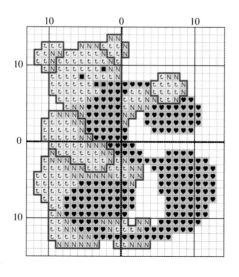

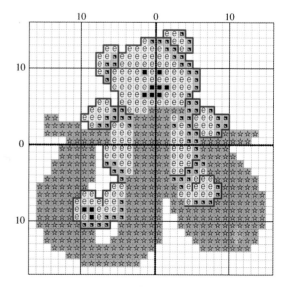

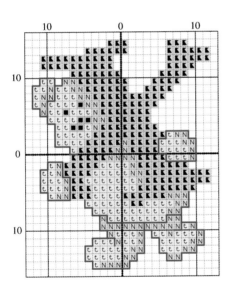

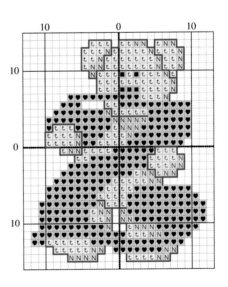

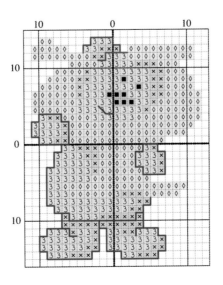

Sporting Bears

Get into action and create these greeting cards decorated with sporting bears! Choose from, clockwise from top left, surfer, golfer, parachuter, cricketer, skate boarder, rugger player, footballer and tennis bears

Worked on a 14 count fabric, each sporting bear is just under 7.5 cm (3 ins) wide and just over 10 cm (4 ins) tall. Opposite are shown the runner and footballer bears, with the other bears on the following four pages. Each chart has its own key shown with it. Although these bears have been used to create greeting cards, they would be ideal to use to decorate a shoe bag or sportsbag.

TEDDY BECKS KEY

★ Cross stitch in two strands

	DMC	Anchor	Madeira	
–	blanc	2	2401	white
♥	350	11	0213	dark red
♡	352	9	0303	red
■	413	400	1713	dark grey
⊿	433	358	2602	dark brown
⊐	436	1045	2011	brown
⋄	727	293	0110	yellow
e	738	367	2013	light brown
⸫	762	234	1804	grey
☾	826	146	1012	dark blue
▼	989	241	1401	green
t	3755	140	1013	blue

★ Backstitch in one strand

	DMC	Anchor	Madeira	
——	413	400	1713	dark grey
——	433	358	2602	dark brown
——	989	241	1401	green

★ STITCH COUNT 54 high x 35 wide

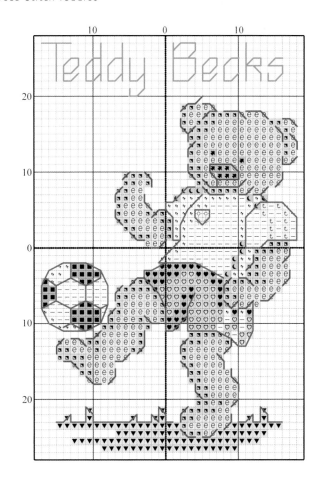

RUGGA BEAR KEY

★ Cross stitch in two strands

	DMC	Anchor	Madeira	
♥	350	11	0213	dark red
♡	352	9	0303	red
⊿	433	358	2602	dark brown
⊐	436	1045	2011	brown
☆	725	305	0108	dark yellow
⋄	727	293	0110	yellow
e	738	367	2013	light brown
☾	826	146	1012	dark blue
▼	989	241	1401	green
t	3755	140	1013	blue
●	3776	1048	2306	ginger

★ Backstitch in one strand

	DMC	Anchor	Madeira	
——	413	400	1713	dark grey
——	433	358	2602	dark brown
——	989	241	1401	green

★ STITCH COUNT 54 high x 35 wide

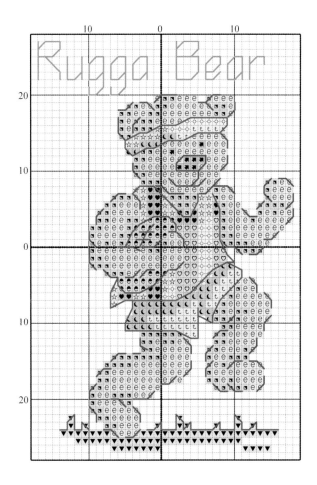

TIGER TEDDY KEY

★ **Cross stitch in two strands**

	DMC	Anchor	Madeira	
♥	350	11	0213	dark red
♡	352	9	0303	red
◢	433	358	2602	dark brown
◩	436	1045	2011	brown
☆	725	305	0108	dark yellow
◌	727	293	0110	yellow
e	738	367	2013	light brown
❟	762	234	1804	grey
☾	826	146	1012	dark blue
∽	827	160	1014	light blue
▼	989	241	1401	green
t	3755	140	1013	blue

★ **Backstitch in one strand**

	DMC	Anchor	Madeira	
——	413	400	1713	dark grey
——	433	358	2602	dark brown
——	989	241	1401	green

★ **STITCH COUNT** 54 high x 35 wide

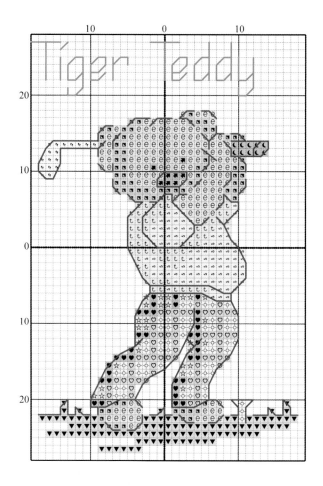

SURF TED KEY

★ Cross stitch in two strands

	DMC	Anchor	Madeira	
–	blanc	2	2402	white
♥	350	11	0213	dark red
♡	352	9	0303	red
◢	433	358	2602	dark brown
◣	436	1045	2011	brown
☆	725	305	0108	dark yellow
◌	727	293	0110	yellow
e	738	367	2013	light brown
∽	827	160	1014	light blue
t	3755	140	1013	blue

★ Backstitch in one strand

——	413	400	1713	dark grey
——	433	358	2602	dark brown
——	826	146	1012	dark blue

★ STITCH COUNT 56 high x 36 wide

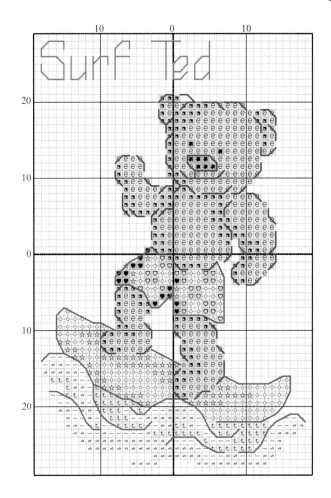

CRICKET BEAR KEY

★ Cross stitch in two strands

	DMC	Anchor	Madeira	
–	blanc	2	2402	white
♥	350	11	0213	dark red
◢	433	358	2602	dark brown
◣	436	1045	2011	brown
☆	725	305	0108	yellow
e	738	367	2013	light brown
⸴	762	234	1804	grey
☾	826	146	1012	dark blue
▼	989	241	1401	green
t	3755	140	1013	blue

★ Backstitch in one strand

——	413	400	1713	dark grey
——	433	358	2602	dark brown
——	989	241	1401	green

★ STITCH COUNT 53 high x 36 wide

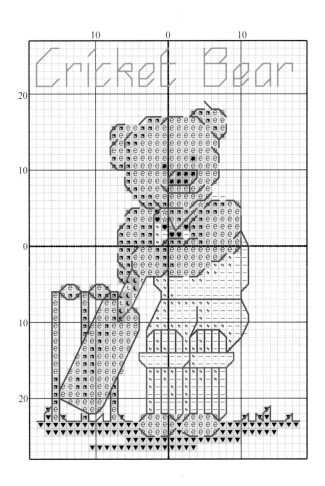

TEDDY HAWKS KEY

★ Cross stitch in two strands

	DMC	Anchor	Madeira	
▽	164	240	1209	light green
♥	350	11	0213	dark red
♡	352	9	0303	red
■	413	400	1713	dark grey
◪	433	358	2602	dark brown
◖	436	1045	2011	brown
☆	725	305	0108	dark yellow
◌	727	293	0110	yellow
e	738	367	2013	light brown
◞	762	234	1804	grey
☾	826	146	1012	dark blue
∽	827	160	1014	light blue
▼	989	241	1401	green
t	3755	140	1013	blue

★ Backstitch in one strand

	DMC	Anchor	Madeira	
——	413	400	1713	dark grey
——	433	358	2602	dark brown
——	826	146	1012	dark blue

★ STITCH COUNT 54 high x 36 wide

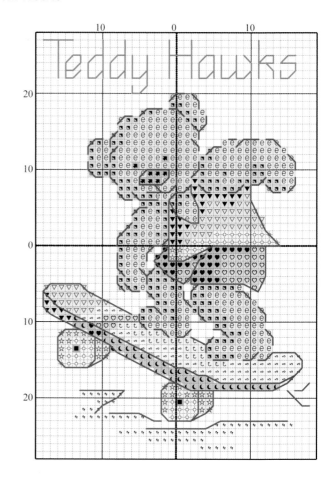

EXTREME TED KEY

★ Cross stitch in two strands

	DMC	Anchor	Madeira	
–	blanc	2	2402	white
♥	350	11	0213	dark red
♡	352	9	0303	red
◪	433	358	2602	dark brown
◖	436	1045	2011	brown
☆	725	305	0108	dark yellow
◌	727	293	0110	yellow
e	738	367	2013	light brown
☾	826	146	1012	dark blue
∽	827	160	1014	light blue
t	3755	140	1013	blue

★ Backstitch in one strand

	DMC	Anchor	Madeira	
——	413	400	1713	dark grey
——	433	358	2602	dark brown
——	826	146	1012	dark blue

★ STITCH COUNT 54 high x 36 wide

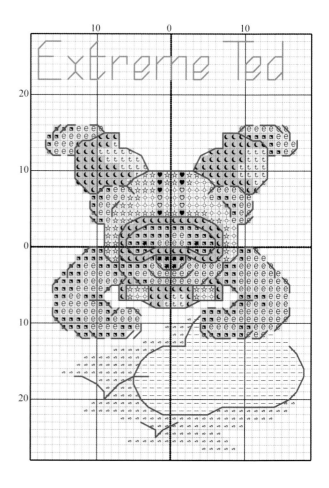

TED HENMAN KEY

★ **Cross stitch in two strands**

	DMC	Anchor	Madeira	
−	blanc	2	2401	white
♥	350	11	0213	dark red
♡	352	9	0303	red
↗	433	358	2602	dark brown
◨	436	1045	2011	brown
e	738	367	2013	light brown
↩	762	234	1804	grey
∽	827	160	1014	light blue
▼	989	241	1401	green
t	3755	140	1013	blue

★ **Backstitch in one strand**

——	413	400	1713	dark grey
——	433	358	2602	dark brown
——	826	146	1012	dark blue
——	989	241	1401	green

★ **STITCH COUNT** 54 high x 36 wide

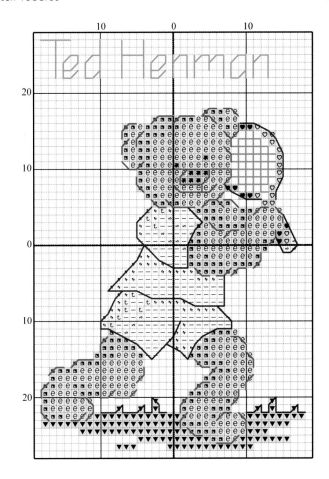

Dear Diary

Mark memorable moments in your life with these cute teddies!

DIARY OF BEARS KEY

★ Cross stitch in two strands

	DMC	Anchor	Madeira	
∩	blanc	2	2402	white
◤	158	177	0912	dark blue
b	208	111	0804	mauve
b	209	109	0803	light mauve
■	310	403	2400	black
◣	350	11	0213	red
я	535	1041	1809	dark grey
e	676	891	2208	straw
▼	703	238	1307	dark green
▽	704	237	1308	green
-ф-	725	305	0108	yellow
e	729	890	2209	dark straw
♡	760	1023	0405	pink
t	761	1021	0404	light pink
I	772	259	1604	light green
∽	819	271	0501	baby pink
◀	869	375	2105	dark tan
☆	922	1003	2306	copper
✎	3072	847	1805	light grey
⊿	3820	306	2509	gold
♥	3831	1025	0508	dark pink
◰	3838	176	2702	blue

★ Backstitch in one strand

	DMC	Anchor	Madeira	
——	310	403	2400	black
——	869	375	2105	dark tan

★ MAXIMUM STITCH COUNT
     55 high x 46 wide

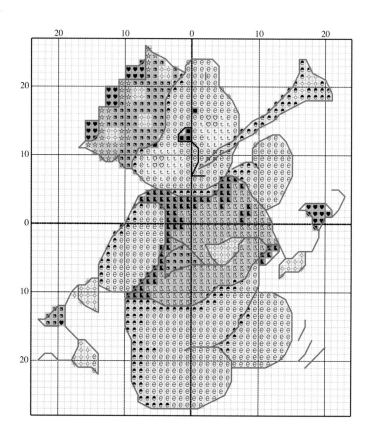

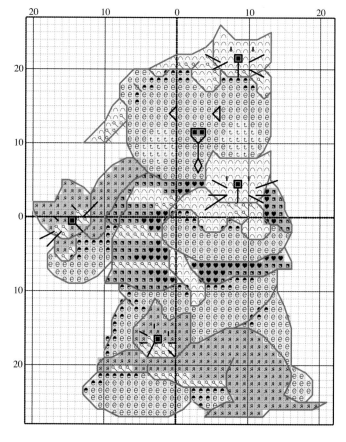

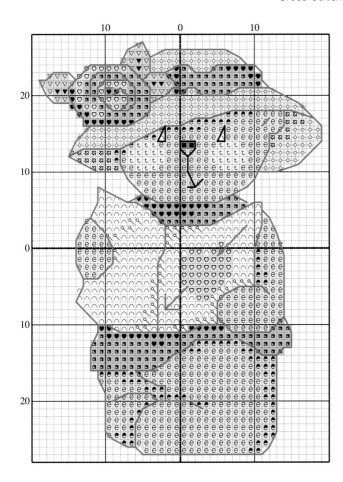

He says he loves me!

I won the biggest sunflower contest

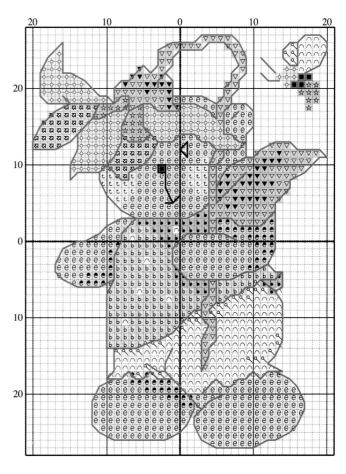

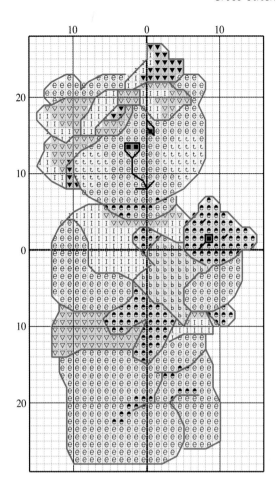

I've got a new teddy!

Oops! Still learning which are the weeds!

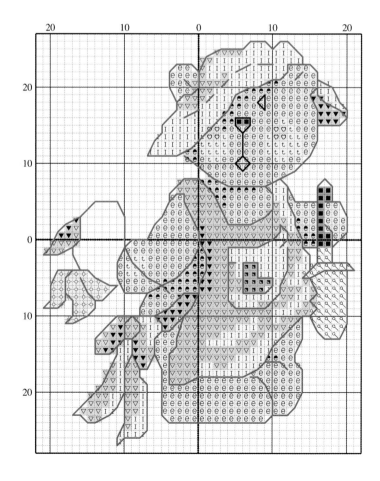

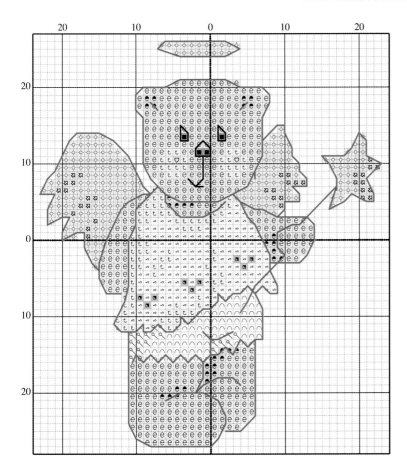

**Mummy said I was
her little angel**

**I'm nervous about
my ballet exam**

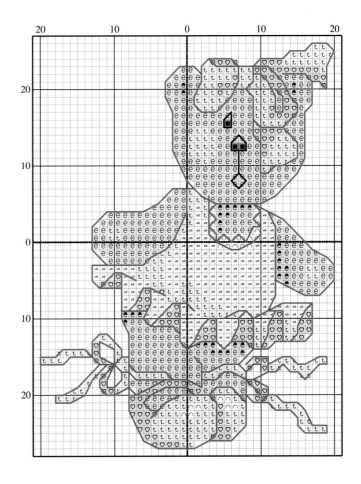

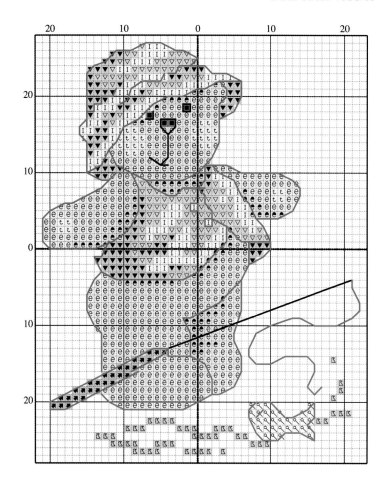

It was this big!

**My new boyfriend
sent me roses!**

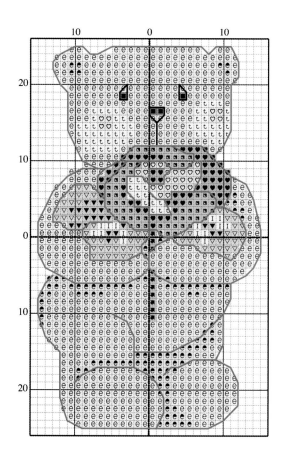

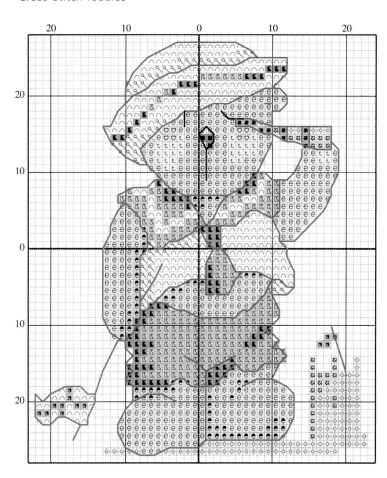

I see no ships!

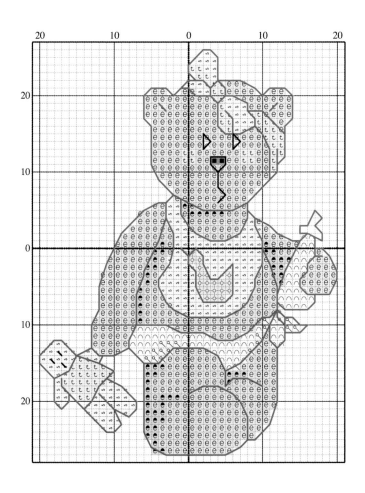

Get well soon

Winter Warmers

*Make cosy gifts to give with the warmest of wishes using these teddy charts.
Choose from the teddies building a snowman on the furry cushion, teddies
having a snowball fight on a hot water bottle cover, or
smiling teddy faces on a comfy pair of slippers*

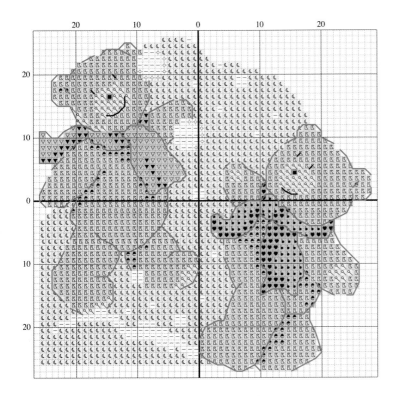

Above: *The teddies having a snow ball fight design, as used on the hot water bottle cover, top left in photograph.*

Worked on a 14 count fabric, this design is about 10 cm (4 ins) square.

TEDDY GIFTS KEY

★ **Cross stitch in two strands**

	DMC	Anchor	Madeira	
–	B5200	1	2401	white
■	310	403	2400	black
♥	347	1025	0407	dark red
♭	349	13	0212	red
K	435	1046	2010	brown
↘	437	362	2012	tan
⚲	676	891	2208	sand
▼	702	226	1306	green
▽	703	238	1307	light green
K	729	890	2209	dark sand
-◇-	746	275	2511	cream
∽	775	1031	1001	light blue
℮	782	308	2212	old gold
⸍	3072	847	1805	grey
♡	3713	1020	0502	pink
☾	3761	120	1001	blue

★ **Backstitch in one strand**

——	310	403	2400	black
——	801	359	2007	dark brown

★ **French knots in two strands**

●	310	403	2400	black

★ **MAXIMUM STITCH COUNT**
   53 high x 55 wide

The key for all charts

Why not make this jolly greeting card, showing sledging teddies, to accompany your hand crafted gift?

The chart for this design is given overleaf

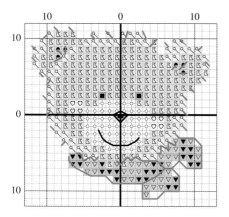

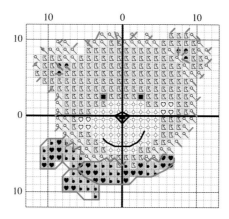

Above: *The smiling teddy faces, as used on the slippers, bottom left in photograph on the previous page and right.*

Worked on a 14 count fabric, each design is about 5 cm (2 ins) square.

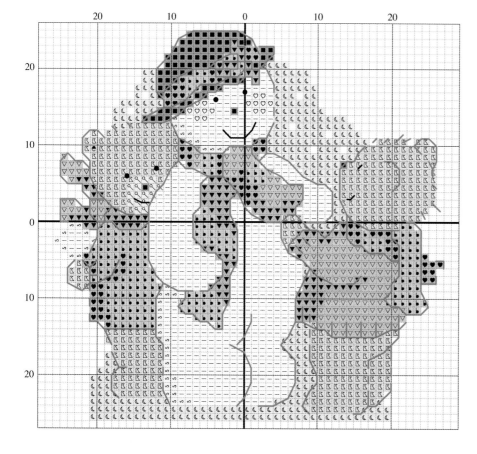

The teddies making a snow man design, as used on the cushion cover, shown above in the photograph on the previous page and above.

Worked on a 14 count fabric, this design is about 10 cm (4 ins) square.

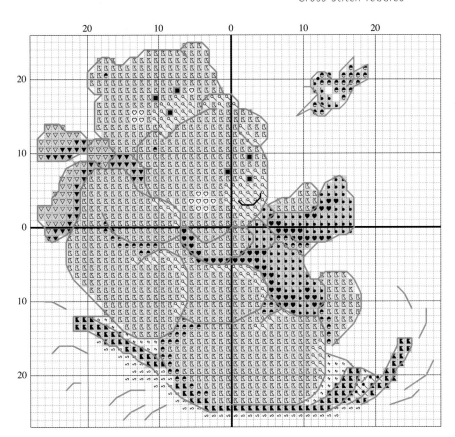

Right: *The teddies sledging design, as used on the greeting card in the photograph below right.*

Worked on a 14 count fabric, this design is about 10 cm (4 ins) square.

TEDDY GIFTS KEY (ALL CHARTS)

★ Cross stitch in two strands

	DMC	Anchor	Madeira	
−	B5200	1	2401	white
■	310	403	2400	black
♥	347	1025	0407	dark red
♭	349	13	0212	red
◪	435	1046	2010	brown
◥	437	362	2012	tan
↙	676	891	2208	sand
▼	702	226	1306	green
▽	703	238	1307	light green
◩	729	890	2209	dark sand
-◇-	746	275	2511	cream
∽	775	1031	1001	light blue
℮	782	308	2212	old gold
↝	3072	847	1805	grey
♡	3713	1020	0502	pink
☾	3761	120	1001	blue

★ Backstitch in one strand

	DMC	Anchor	Madeira	
———	310	403	2400	black
———	801	359	2007	dark brown

★ French knots in two strands

	DMC	Anchor	Madeira	
●	310	403	2400	black

★ MAXIMUM STITCH COUNT
53 high x 55 wide

Timeless Teddies

Make this stunning picture to adorn the nursery wall

TIMELESS TEDDIES KEY

★ **Cross stitch in two strands**

	DMC	Anchor	Madeira	
—	blanc	2	2402	white
◊	164	203	1210	green
■	310	403	2400	black
♥	347	13	0407	dark red
♭	351	10	0214	red
◤	434	310	2008	dark brown
◳	435	1046	2010	brown
◰	436	1045	2011	light brown
e	437	362	2012	light tan
⚲	613	831	2109	beige
N	676	891	2208	sand
я	677	852	2207	light sand
▽	704	255	1308	lime green
e	729	890	2209	dark sand
★	742	303	0201	tangerine
☆	743	302	0113	yellow
⌖	744	295	0112	light yellow
⸙	746	386	2511	cream
ᔕ	772	259	1604	light green
✳	797	147	0912	dark blue
☾	798	137	0911	blue
☽	799	145	0910	light blue
▼	905	257	1412	dark green
♡	963	23	0502	very light pink
◓	3023	900	1902	grey
∩	3072	847	1805	light grey
J	3326	36	0612	light pink
♭	3712	10	0406	pink
⇗	3829	901	2213	dark straw
t	3840	144	0907	very light blue

★ **Backstitch in one strand**

——	310	403	2400	black
——	433	944	2007	dark brown

★ **STITCH COUNT** 110 high x 208 wide

Right: *The chart for this stunning picture, featuring teddies and toys, reminiscent of days gone by.*

Worked on a 14 count fabric, this design is just over 20 cm (8 ins) tall and just under 42 cm (16 ins) wide.

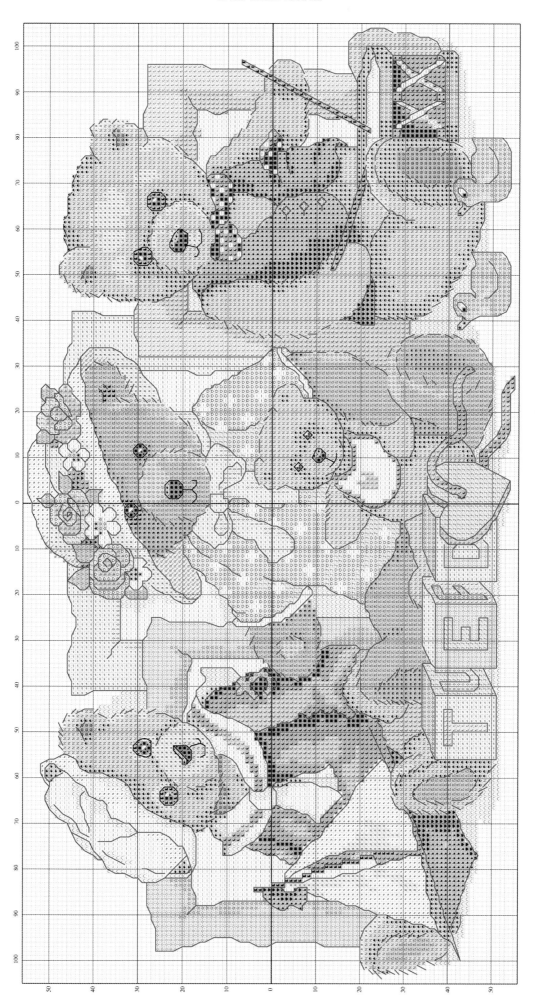

Bears by Numbers

Use these numbers to decorate baby clothes - there's a version of every number for a girl and a boy!

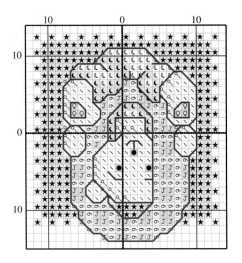

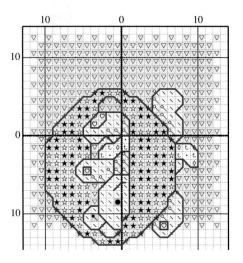

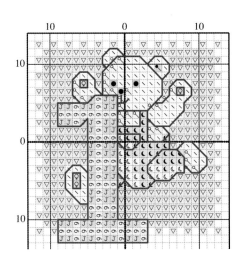

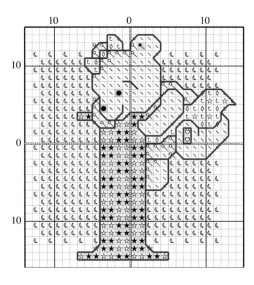

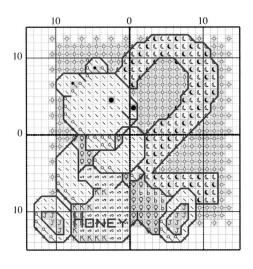

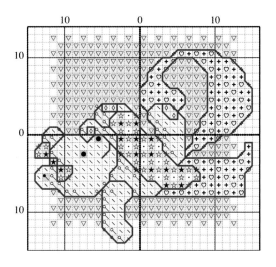

TEDDY NUMBERS KEY

★ Cross stitch in two strands			
	DMC	**Anchor**	**Madeira**	
·	blanc	2	2402	white
◇	209	109	0803	mauve
t	211	342	0801	light mauve
▽	340	118	0902	violet
➘	435	1046	2010	brown
⚲	437	362	2012	light brown
∽	676	891	2208	sand
J	703	238	1307	green
3	726	295	0109	yellow
Κ	729	890	2209	dark sand
＼	738	942	2013	beige
⋄̇	742	303	0114	orange
b	813	140	0910	light blue
♀	826	146	0906	blue
♡	894	31	0414	pink
●	898	360	2006	dark brown
☽	954	203	1207	light green
☾	958	187	1114	mint green
+	963	73	0502	light pink
☾	964	185	1112	lt mint green
★	3340	329	0301	peach
☆	3341	328	0302	light peach
★ Backstitch in one strand			
——	898	360	2006	dark brown

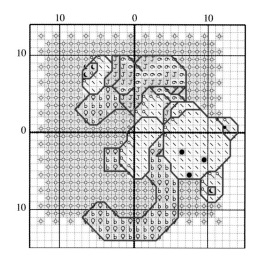

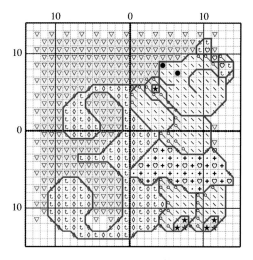

On a 14 count fabric, each design isabout 5 cm (2 ins) tall.

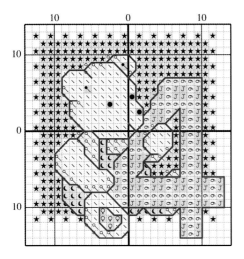

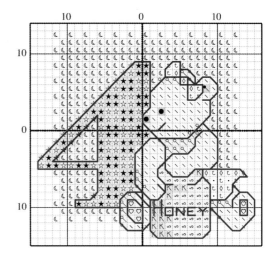

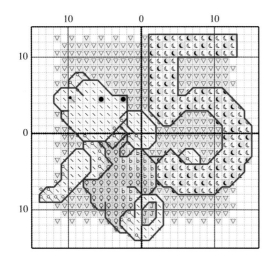

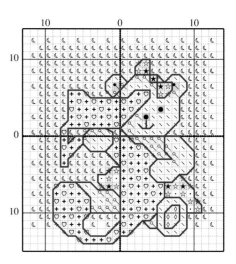

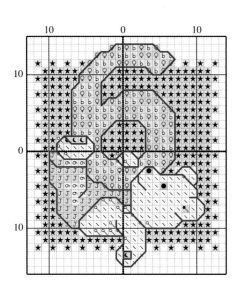

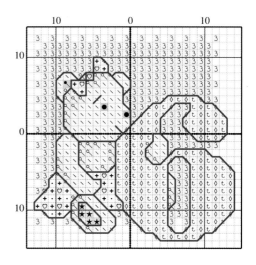

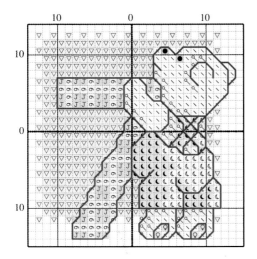

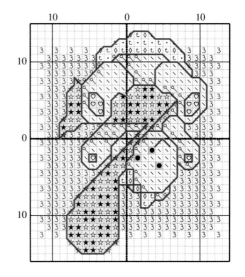

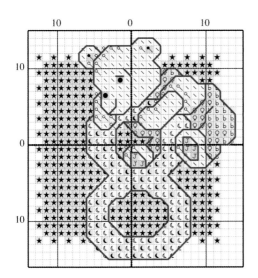

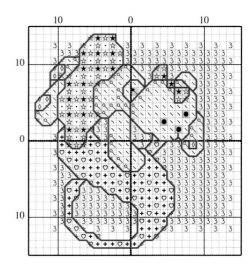

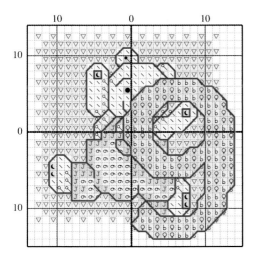

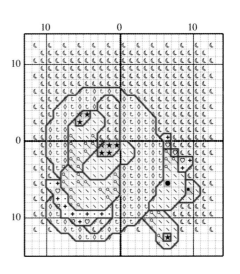

Month by month

Make a bear of every month of the year with these charts

JANEY TED KEY (JANUARY)

★ Cross stitch in two strands

	DMC	Anchor	Madeira	
e	208	111	0804	lilac
e	209	109	0803	light lilac
↗	433	358	2008	brown
3	745	300	0111	yellow
■	938	380	2206	dark brown
v	3046	887	2206	straw
◑	3820	306	2509	gold
◌	3822	295	2511	light gold
▼	3828	373	2103	tan

★ Cross stitch in one strand of each colour

	DMC	Anchor	Madeira	
▽	3046/3828	887/373	2206/2103	straw/tan

★ Backstitch in one strand

	DMC	Anchor	Madeira	
——	347	1025	0407	red
——	433	358	2008	brown
——	938	380	2005	dark brown

★ STITCH COUNT 52 high x 37 wide

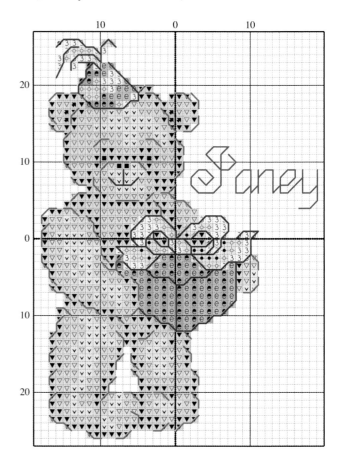

CHARLIE TED KEY (FEBRUARY)

★ Cross stitch in two strands

	DMC	Anchor	Madeira	
e	334	977	1004	dark blue
♥	347	1025	0407	red
☙	367	217	1312	green
↗	433	358	2008	brown
3	775	1031	1001	light blue
♦	938	380	2206	dark brown
я	3046	887	2206	straw
e	3325	129	0907	blue
♡	3712	1023	0406	pink
◌	3820	306	2509	gold
+	3822	295	2511	light gold
♭	3828	373	2103	tan

★ Cross stitch in one strand of each colour

	DMC	Anchor	Madeira	
☐	3046/3828	887/373	2206/2103	straw/tan

★ Backstitch in one strand

	DMC	Anchor	Madeira	
——	347	1025	0407	red
——	433	358	2008	brown
——	938	380	2005	dark brown

★ STITCH COUNT 51 high x 39 wide

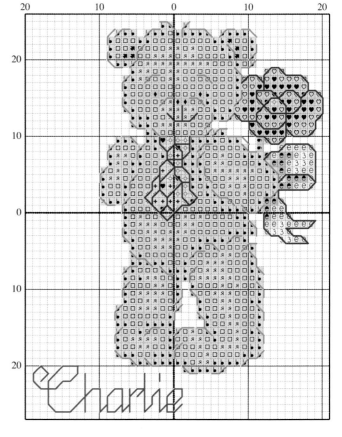

PERCY TED KEY (MARCH)

★ **Cross stitch in two strands**

	DMC	Anchor	Madeira	
☆	blanc	2	2402	white
☉	208	111	0804	lilac
℮	209	109	0803	light lilac
✛	319	1044	1313	dark green
♥	347	1025	0407	red
◗	367	217	1312	green
∽	368	214	1310	light green
✳	415	398	1802	grey
➐	433	358	2008	brown
♦	646	8581	1812	dark grey
◇	647	1040	1813	ash grey
●	938	380	2206	dark brown
∨	3046	887	2206	straw
♡	3712	1023	0406	pink
◔	3820	306	2509	gold
◌	3822	295	2511	light gold
▼	3828	373	2103	tan

★ **Cross stitch in one strand of each colour**

$	3046/3828	887/373	2206/2103	straw/tan

★ **Backstitch in one strand**

——	347	1025	0407	red
——	433	358	2008	brown
——	938	380	2005	dark brown

★ **STITCH COUNT** 45 high x 40 wide

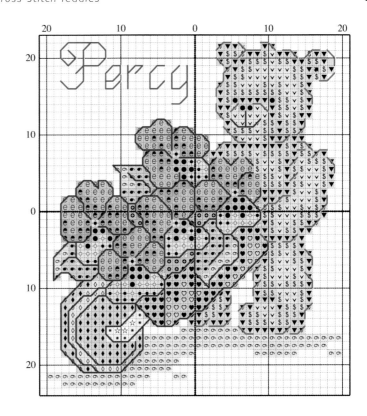

APRIL TED KEY (APRIL)

★ **Cross stitch in two strands**

	DMC	Anchor	Madeira	
☉	208	111	0804	lilac
℮	209	109	0803	light lilac
♥	347	1025	0407	red
➐	433	358	2008	brown
♦	646	8581	1812	dark grey
◇	647	1040	1813	ash grey
●	938	380	2206	dark brown
×	3046	887	2206	straw
♡	3712	1023	0406	pink
◔	3820	306	2509	gold
◌	3822	295	2511	light gold
▼	3828	373	2103	tan

★ **Cross stitch in one strand of each colour**

∨	3046/3828	887/373	2206/2103	straw/tan

★ **Backstitch in one strand**

——	347	1025	0407	red
——	433	358	2008	brown
——	938	380	2005	dark brown

★ **STITCH COUNT** 55 high x 48 wide

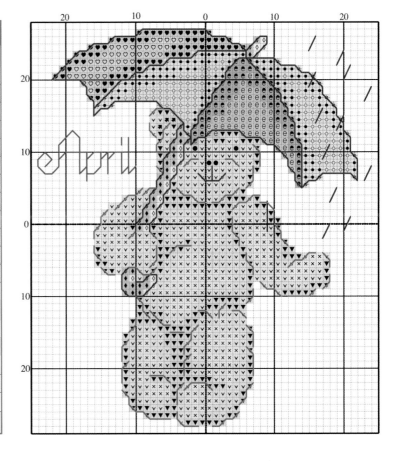

MARY TED KEY (MAY)

★ Cross stitch in two strands

	DMC	Anchor	Madeira	
e	208	111	0804	lilac
e	209	109	0803	light lilac
●	367	217	1312	green
ง	368	214	1310	light green
ง	415	398	1802	grey
⌐	433	358	2008	brown
♦	646	8581	1812	dark grey
◊	647	1040	1813	ash grey
3	745	300	0111	yellow
●	938	380	2206	dark brown
v	3046	887	2206	straw
♡	3712	1023	0406	pink
◈	3820	306	2509	gold
▼	3828	373	2103	tan

★ Cross stitch in one strand of each colour

	DMC	Anchor	Madeira	
×	3046/3828	887/373	2206/2103	straw/tan

★ Backstitch in one strand

	DMC	Anchor	Madeira	
——	433	358	2008	brown
——	938	380	2005	dark brown

★ STITCH COUNT 46 high x 37 wide

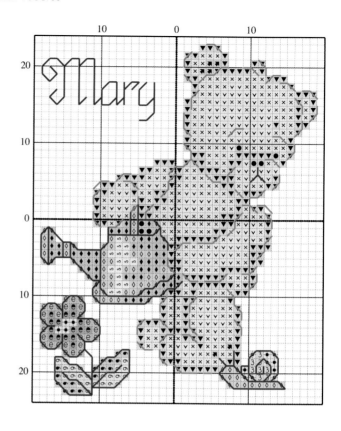

HARRY TED KEY (JUNE)

★ Cross stitch in two strands

	DMC	Anchor	Madeira	
∩	blanc	2	2402	white
я	334	977	1004	dark blue
●	367	217	1312	green
ง	368	215	1310	light green
+	415	498	1802	grey
3	745	300	0111	gold
v	3046	887	2206	straw
♀	3325	129	0907	blue
◈	3822	295	2511	light gold
▼	3828	373	2103	tan

★ Cross stitch in one strand of each colour

	DMC	Anchor	Madeira	
×	3046/3828	887/373	2206/2103	straw/tan

★ Backstitch in one strand

	DMC	Anchor	Madeira	
——	347	1025	0407	red
——	433	358	2008	brown
——	938	380	2005	dark brown

★ STITCH COUNT 43 high x 41 wide

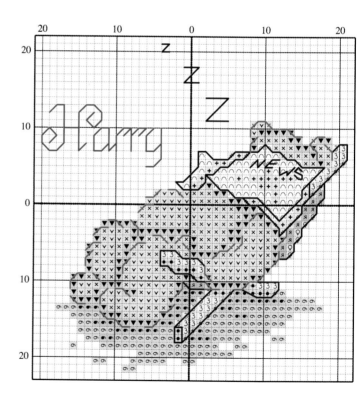

SAM TED KEY (JULY)

★ **Cross stitch in two strands**

	DMC	Anchor	Madeira	
∩	blanc	2	2402	white
я	334	977	1004	dark blue
♥	347	1025	0407	red
+	415	498	1802	grey
➚	433	358	2008	brown
3	775	1031	1001	light blue
●	938	380	2206	dark brown
v	3046	887	2206	straw
♀	3325	129	0907	blue
♡	3712	1023	0406	pink
▼	3828	373	2103	tan

★ **Cross stitch in one strand of each colour**

×	3046/3828	887/373	2206/2103	straw/tan

★ **Backstitch in one strand**

———	347	1025	0407	red
———	433	358	2008	brown
———	938	380	2005	dark brown

★ **STITCH COUNT** 56 high x 36 wide

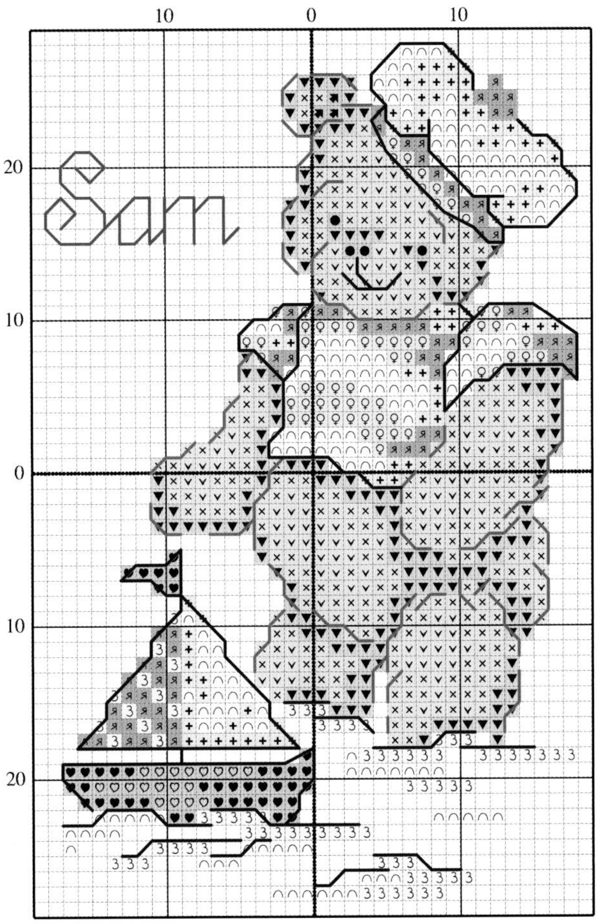

TILLY TED KEY (AUGUST)

★ **Cross stitch in two strands**

	DMC	Anchor	Madeira	
♥	347	1025	0407	red
➚	433	358	2008	brown
3	745	300	0111	yellow
☾	775	1031	1001	light blue
●	938	380	2206	dark brown
v	3046	887	2206	straw
♀	3325	129	0907	blue
♡	3712	1023	0406	pink
-●-	3820	306	2509	gold
-○-	3822	295	2511	light gold
▼	3828	373	2103	tan

★ **Cross stitch in one strand of each colour**

×	3046/3828	887/373	2206/2103	straw/tan

★ **Backstitch in one strand**

———	347	1025	0407	red
———	433	358	2008	brown
———	938	380	2005	dark brown

★ **STITCH COUNT** 50 high x 37 wide

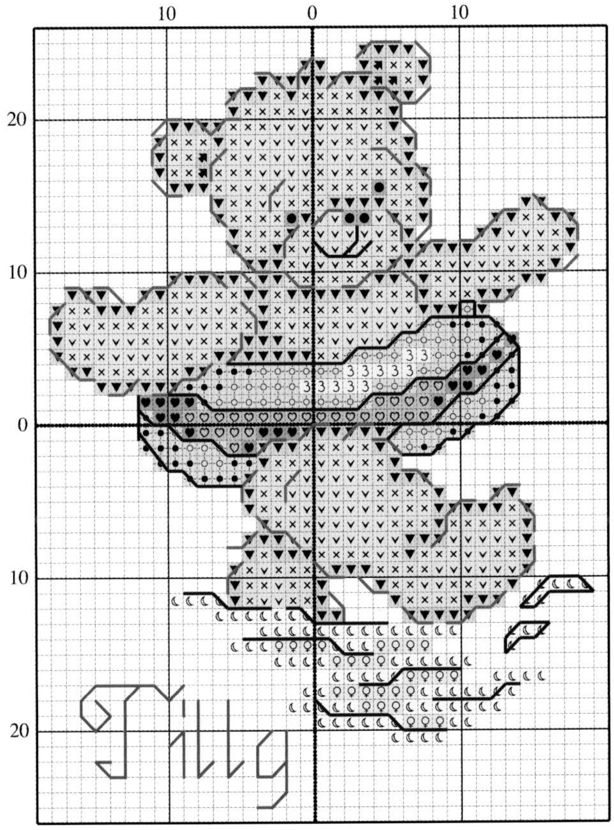

SEBASTIAN TED KEY (SEPT)

★ **Cross stitch in two strands**

	DMC	Anchor	Madeira	
∩	blanc	2	2402	white
❤	347	1025	0407	red
✎	367	217	1312	green
♍	368	214	1310	light green
I	415	398	1802	grey
⚑	433	358	2008	brown
♦	646	8581	1812	dark ash grey
◊	647	1040	1813	ash grey
ᔑ	775	1031	1001	light blue
♦	938	380	2206	dark brown
+	3046	887	2206	straw
-●-	3325	129	0907	blue
-◇-	3712	1023	0406	pink
▼	3828	373	2103	tan

★ **Cross stitch in one strand of each colour**

ᵛ	3046/3828	887/373	2206/2103	straw/tan

★ **Backstitch in one strand**

——	347	1025	0407	red
——	433	358	2008	brown
——	938	380	2005	dark brown

★ **STITCH COUNT** 47 high x 41 wide

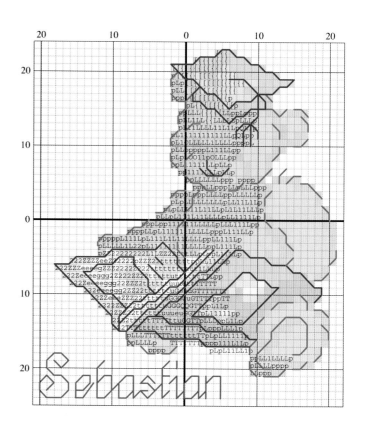

TAMMY TED KEY (OCT)

★ **Cross stitch in two strands**

	DMC	Anchor	Madeira	
╲	blanc	2	2402	white
∩	415	398	1802	grey
☾	745	300	0111	light yellow
ᔑ	775	1031	1001	blue
♦	938	380	2206	dark brown
+	3046	887	2206	straw
-●-	3820	306	2509	gold
-◇-	3822	295	2511	light gold
▼	3828	373	2103	tan

★ **Cross stitch in one strand of each colour**

ᵛ	3046/3828	887/373	2206/2103	straw/tan

★ **Backstitch in one strand**

——	347	1025	0407	red
——	433	358	2008	brown
——	938	380	2005	dark brown

★ **STITCH COUNT** 47 high x 47 wide

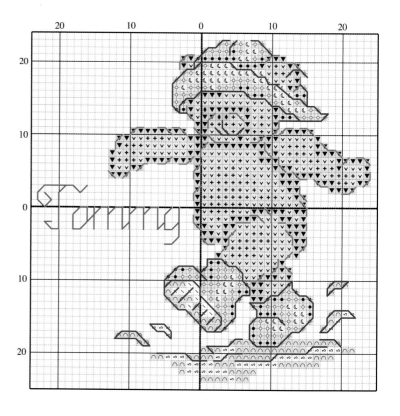

JACK TED KEY (NOV)

★ **Cross stitch in two strands**

	DMC	Anchor	Madeira	
●	367	217	1312	green
ᵔ	368	214	1310	light green
◤	433	358	2008	brown
●	938	380	2206	dark brown
v	3046	887	2206	straw
▼	3828	373	2103	tan

★ **Cross stitch in one strand of each colour**

	DMC	Anchor	Madeira	
∽	3046/3828	887/373	2206/2103	straw/tan

★ **Backstitch in one strand**

	DMC	Anchor	Madeira	
——	319	1044	1313	dark green
——	347	1025	0407	red
——	433	358	2008	brown
——	938	380	2005	dark brown

★ **STITCH COUNT** 42 high x 41 wide

NOEL TED KEY (DEC)

★ **Cross stitch in two strands**

	DMC	Anchor	Madeira	
∩	blanc	2	2402	white
e	208	111	0804	lilac
✿	319	1044	1313	dark green
♥	347	1025	0407	red
●	367	217	1312	green
I	415	398	1802	grey
◤	433	358	2008	brown
3	745	300	0111	yellow
●	938	380	2206	dark brown
∽	3046	887	2206	straw
♡	3712	1023	0406	pink
◉	3820	306	2509	gold
◌	3822	295	2511	light gold
▼	3828	373	2103	tan

★ **Cross stitch in one strand of each colour**

	DMC	Anchor	Madeira	
v	3046/3828	887/373	2206/2103	straw/tan

★ **Backstitch in one strand**

	DMC	Anchor	Madeira	
——	347	1025	0407	red
——	433	358	2008	brown
——	938	380	2005	dark brown

★ **STITCH COUNT** 49 high x 45 wide

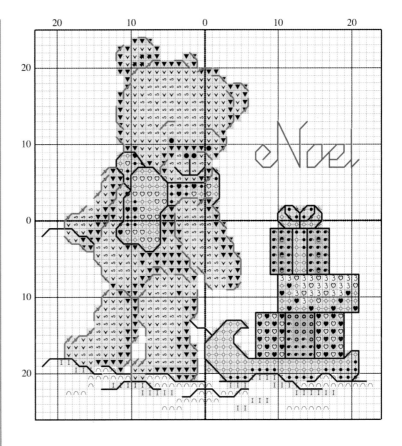

Teds for all Seasons

*Make this clever sampler-style framed picture featuring
a different type of ted for each season! You've got a ted in
his neat souwester for spring, one with his bear-sized
sunflower depicting summer, a jolly ted frolicking in
the leaves for autumn, and a santa-style ted for winter*

Worked on a 14 count fabric, the completed "Teds For All Seasons" picture measures about 20 cm (8 ins) square, including the floral border and message across the bottom.

Frame your picture as we have here, without a mount board and inside a toning wood-effect frame, or make it a larger "work of art" by using a wide mount board and a much bigger frame. The big frame does not have to be square – so long as the hole cut in the mount board is the right shape! Pick out one of the soft shades within the embroidery for the colour of the mount board, or use classic cream, and perhaps choose one of the stronger tones for the frame.

If you prefer, you can work each season separately and frame all four as smaller seasonal pictures - or make just one. If you

decide to make all four, try framing them all the same and hanging them in a group to create your own version of a "Ted For All Seasons". Either hang them all in a line, or form them into a big square, placing them in two rows of two pictures, one on top of the other.

As the completed picture, featuring all four seasons, is about 20 cm (8 ins) square, each separate season will easily fit into a 10 cm (4 ins) square when worked on a 14 count fabric.

Below: *The key for the chart, shown overleaf.*

TEDS FOR ALL SEASONS KEY

★ Cross stitch in two strands

	DMC	Anchor	Madeira	
·	blanc	2	2402	white
⋄	307	289	0104	yellow
÷	318	399	1801	grey
♫	341	117	0901	violet blue
○	351	10	0214	red
☾	433	358	2602	dark tan
☆	435	1046	2010	tan
☾	437	362	2012	light tan
♦	469	267	1503	dark green
▽	470	266	1502	green
◇	471	265	1501	light green
♡	760	1022	0405	pink
★	801	359	2007	brown
∨	813	140	0910	light blue
℮	817	13	0210	dark red
⚑	824	143	1010	dark blue
∽	826	146	0906	blue
3	922	1003	2306	ginger
⊙	972	298	0107	dark yellow
♥	3328	1024	0406	dark pink
★ Backstitch in one strand				
——	838	380	2005	dark brown
★ STITCH COUNT 60 high x 60 wide				

Make the complete "Teds For All Seasons" picture, as shown above, or embroider just one of the seasons on its own.

Make each separate season into a little framed picture, like the "Spring" picture shown on the previous page, or use it to decorate other items around the home. Here we have used "Summer" to decorate a jolly note pad holder.

You could use them as greeting card designs too!

The chart for the complete "Teds For All Seasons" picture.

The key is shown on page 90.

Summer Fun
Alphabet Bears

Use these clever, fun-filled bear letters to decorate items for your holiday!
Add a whole name, as shown below, or just one letter
to give something that special personal touch

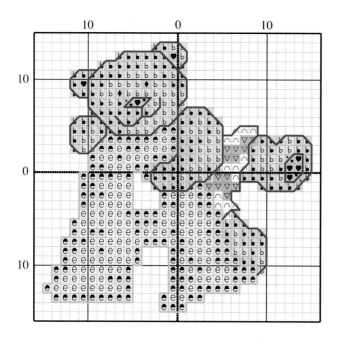

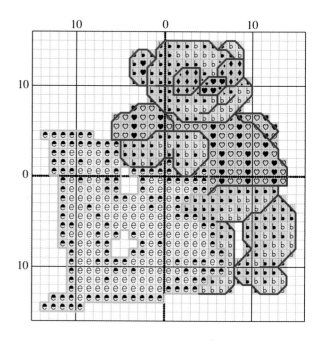

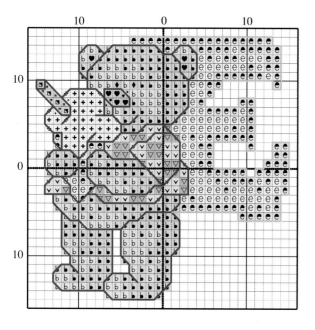

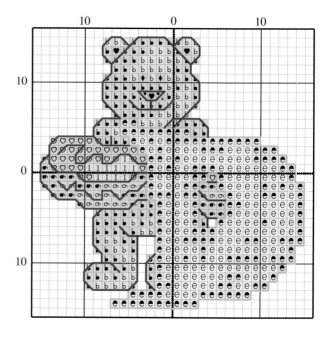

SUMMER TEDS ABC KEY

★ Cross stitch in two strands

	DMC	Anchor	Madeira	
∩	blanc	2	2402	white
$	340	118	0902	mauve
♡	350	11	0213	red
I	352	9	0303	light red
♥	355	1014	2501	brick red
◣	433	358	2602	brown
+	605	50	0613	pink
e	676	891	2208	light sand
◔	702	226	1306	dark green
∽	704	237	1308	green
℮	729	890	2209	sand
▼	797	139	0913	dark blue
▽	798	137	0912	blue
∨	799	145	0910	light blue
○	955	206	1210	light green
♦	3031	360	2003	dark brown
◖	3863	379	1912	dark beige
b	3864	376	1910	beige

★ Backstitch in one strand

——	350	11	0213	red
——	680	901	2210	dark sand
——	3031	360	2003	dark brown

★ MAXIMUM STITCH COUNT
30 high x 35 wide

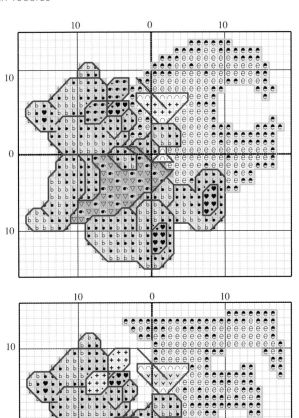

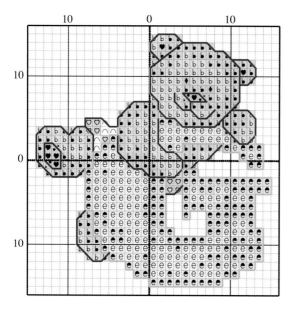

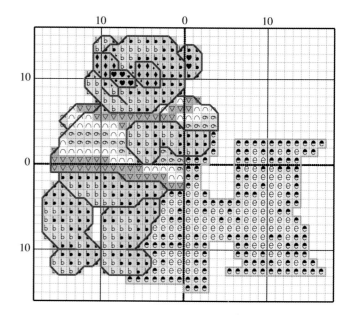

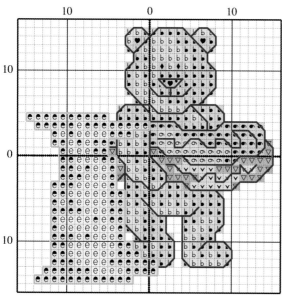

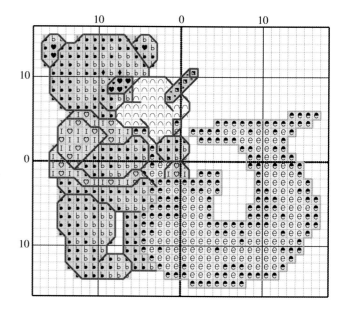

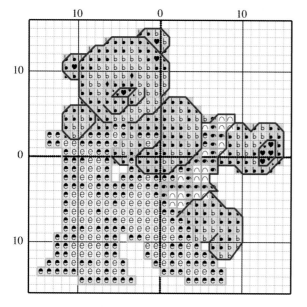

On pages 96-97 are the charts for letters A to F, here you have letters G to P, and overleaf are letters Q to Z.

When worked on a 14 count fabric, each letter is just over 5 cm (2 ins) tall.

The key for all the letters is shown on the previous page.

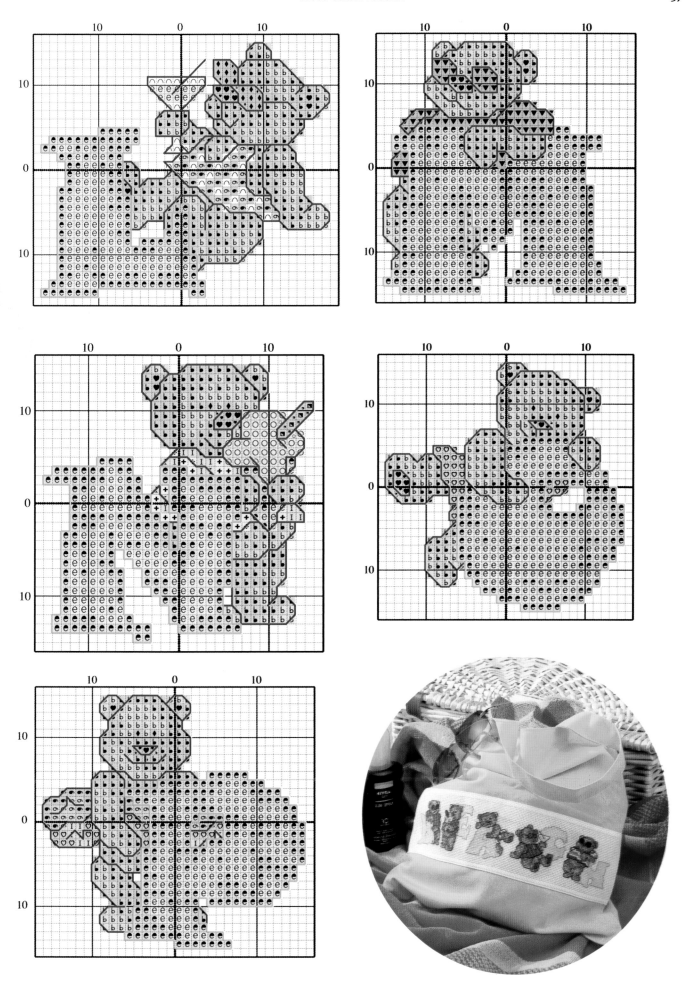

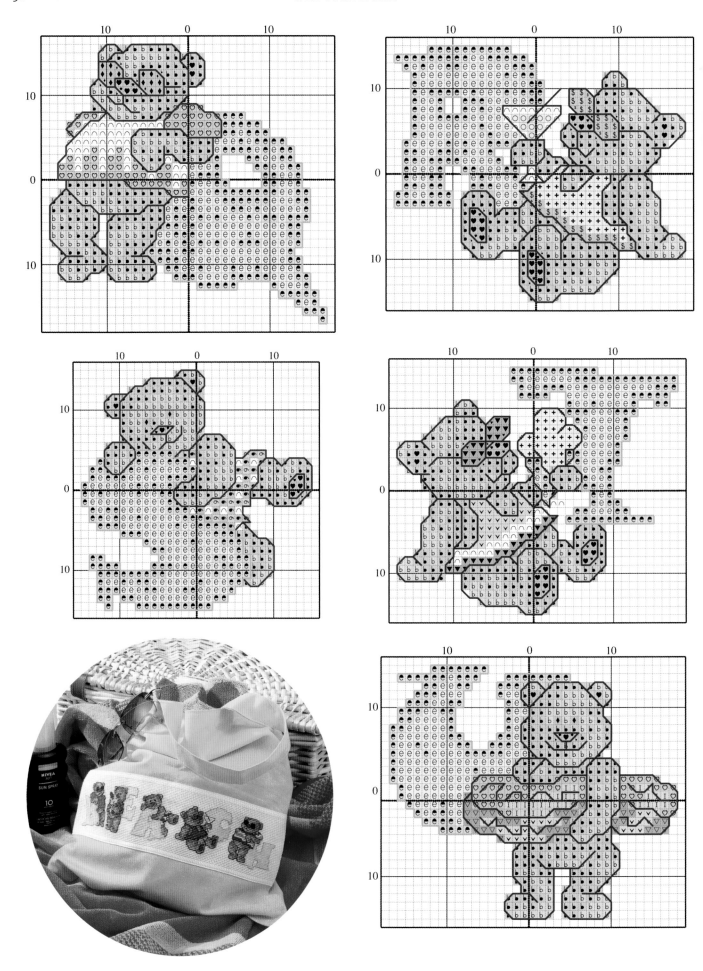

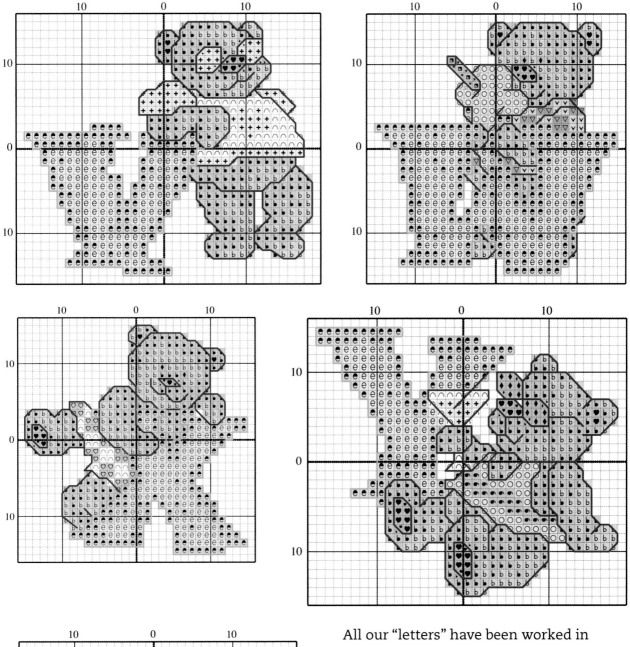

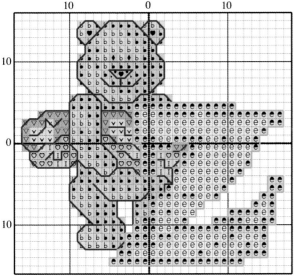

All our "letters" have been worked in sunny yellow - but you could choose any colour to match with the item it is to be used on. But, whatever colour you choose, make sure it will not clash with the other colours within the ted!

The key for all the letters is shown on pages 96-97.

Beautiful Baby Bears

*Create this beautiful sampler picture to commemorate
a baby's birth – or make the little picture to hang on
the newborn's nursery wall. Complete the trio
with the jolly greeting card design*

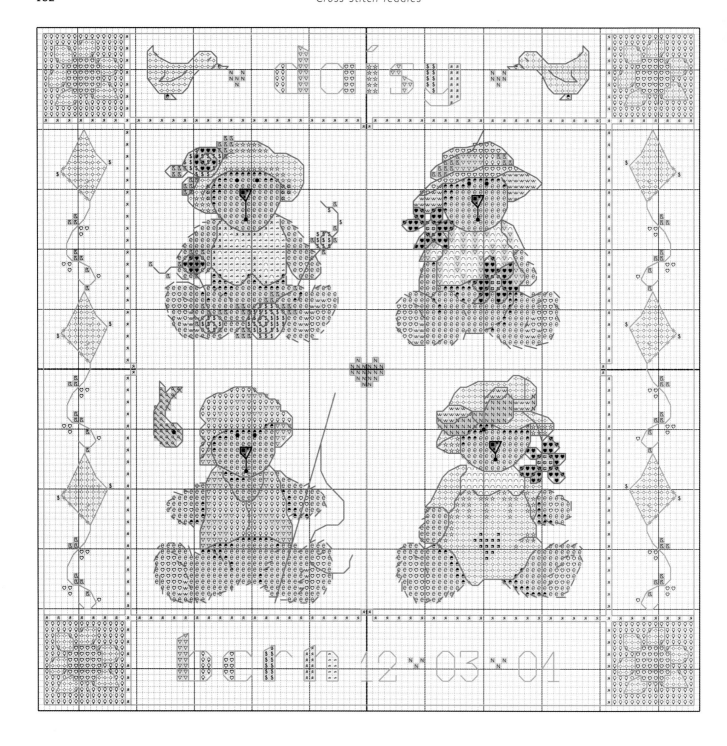

Above: *The chart for the sampler picture.*

Opposite middle right: *The greeting card chart.*

Opposite, bottom: *Use these letters to add your special name to the sampler.*

Opposite, left: *The key for all charts.*

Opposite, top right: *The chart for the little mini-picture.*

TEDDY BIRTH SAMPLER KEY

★ **Cross stitch in two strands**

	DMC	Anchor	Madeira	
▽	164	240	1209	green
я	210	108	0802	lilac
ﻝ	211	342	0801	light lilac
■	310	403	2400	black
♀	369	1043	1309	light green
⚲	647	1040	1812	grey
e	676	891	2208	sand
К	703	238	1307	bright green
⤳	728	305	0107	dark yellow
◖	729	890	2209	dark sand
☆	744	301	0112	yellow
◣	962	75	0609	dark pink
♡	963	73	0502	light pink
⦿	3078	292	0102	light yellow
w	3326	36	0606	pink
♥	3607	87	0708	cerise
$	3608	86	0709	light cerise
N	3712	1023	0406	coral
∩	3865	2	2403	white

★ **Backstitch in one strand**

	DMC	Anchor	Madeira	
——	310	403	2400	black
——	553	98	0712	mauve
——	869	375	2105	brown

★ **French knots in one strand**

	DMC	Anchor	Madeira	
●	310	403	2400	black

★ **STITCH COUNT** - main picture
    112 high x 112 wide

★ **STITCH COUNT** - small picture
    39 high x 36 wide

★ **STITCH COUNT** - card
    27 high x 21 wide

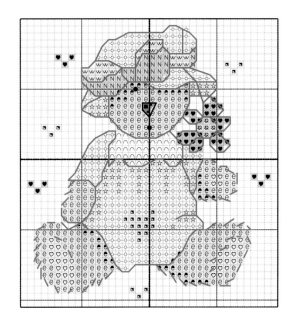

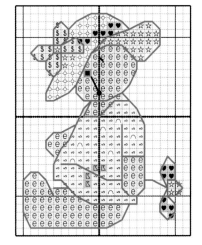

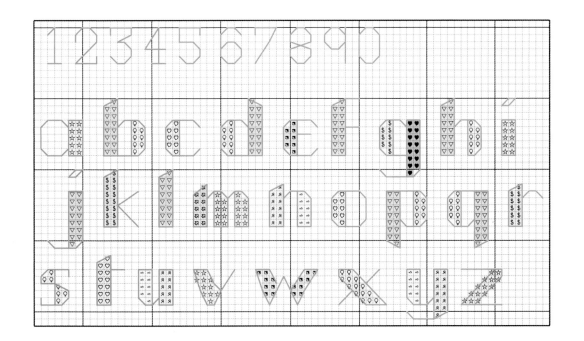

It's play time!

*Use these jolly charts to add a playful touch to your work.
Make them into greeting cards, add them onto aprons, embroider
them onto bibs, or sprinkle them onto cushions and covers – you are
bound to have just as much fun as these bears are!*

The key for all these charts, and those shown on the following two pages, is given on page 107.

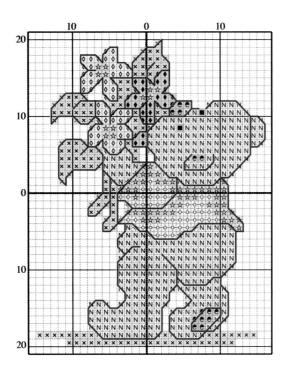

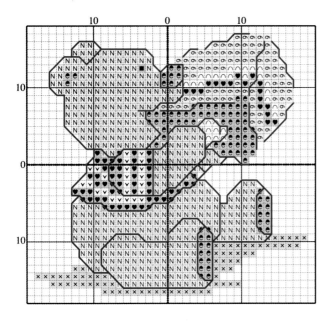

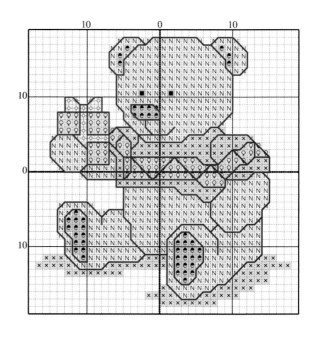

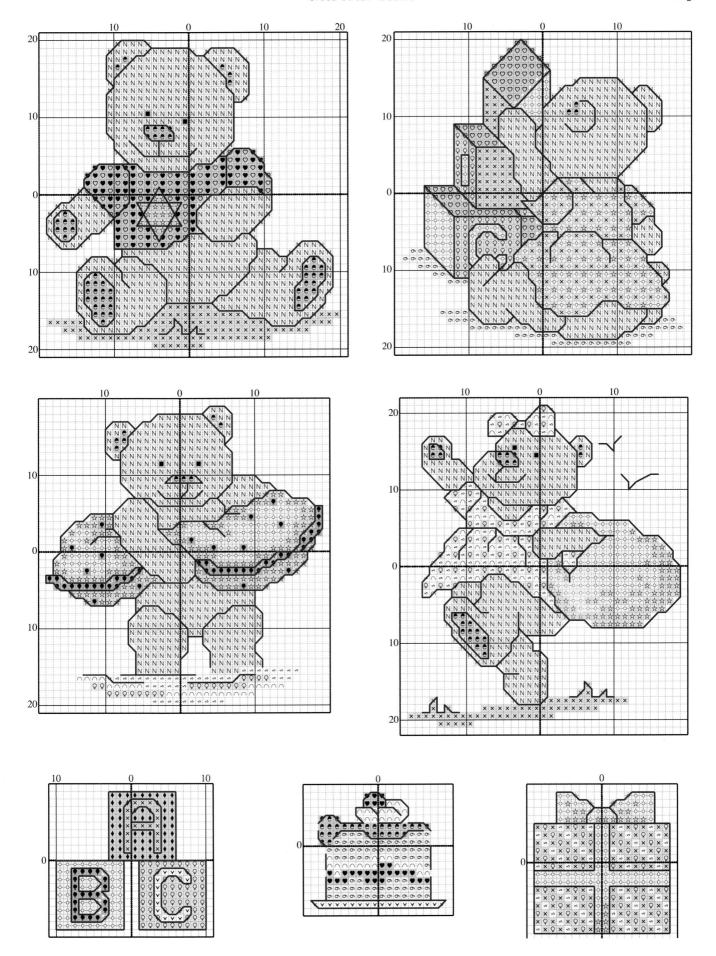

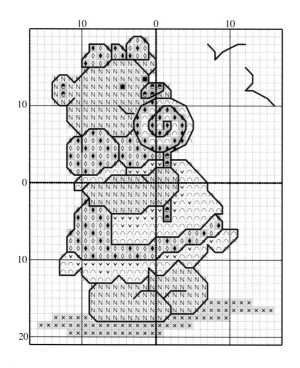

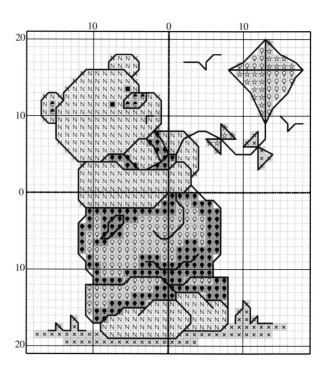

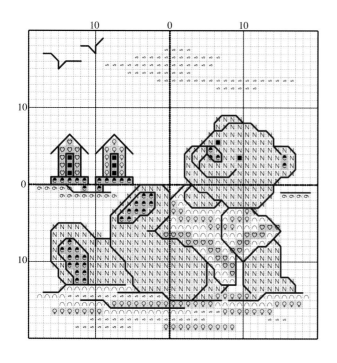

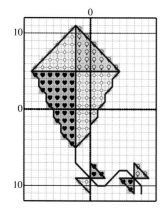

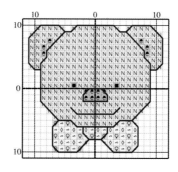

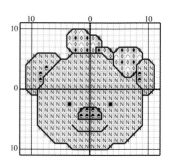

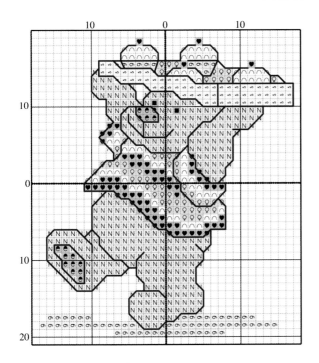

PLAYFUL TEDS KEY

★ Cross stitch in two strands

	DMC	Anchor	Madeira	
∩	blanc	2	2402	white
♥	349	13	0212	red
♡	351	10	0214	light red
℮	434	310	2009	brown
N	437	362	2012	light brown
ჟ	676	891	2208	sand
×	704	237	1308	green
☆	742	303	0114	tangerine
·◇·	744	301	0112	yellow
∨	762	234	1804	light grey
♥	798	137	0912	dark blue
♀	799	145	0910	blue
ᔕ	800	144	0908	light blue
♦	956	40	0506	pink
◊	957	50	0504	light pink
■	3371	382	2004	dark brown

★ Backstitch in one strand

	DMC	Anchor	Madeira	
——	3371	382	2004	dark brown

★ MAXIMUM STITCH COUNT
42 high x 40 wide

The key for all these charts, and those shown on the previous two pages, is shown above.

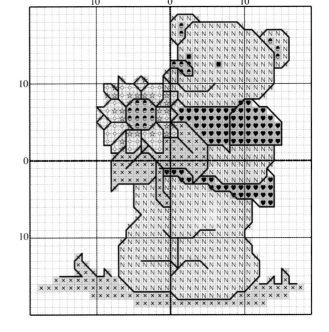

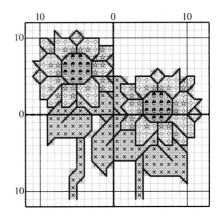

Yoga Bears

Get in touch with your inner bear and embroider these cute teds in classic yoga poses. Use them to decorate your sports towel – or as little pictures to frame and hang on the wall. Or perhaps you could use one on a greeting card for a yoga-loving friend?

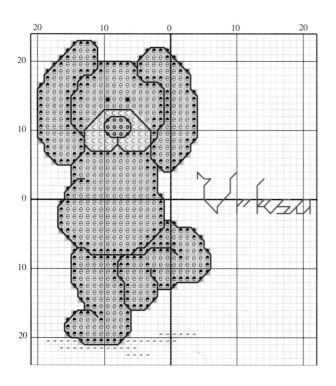

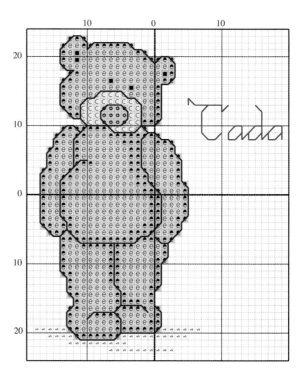

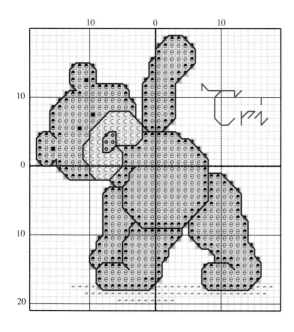

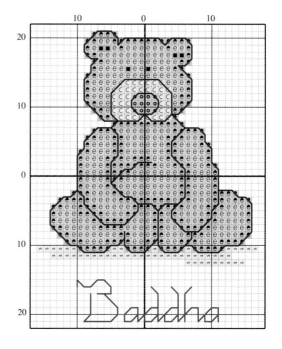

YOGA BEARS KEY

★ **Cross stitch in two strands**

	DMC	Anchor	Madeira	
✪	355	1014	2501	brick red
●	435	1046	2010	brown
e	436	1045	2011	light brown
C	738	367	2013	light tan
ʃ	800	144	0908	light blue
■	898	360	2006	dark brown

★ **Backstitch in one strand**

	798	146	0911	blue
——	898	360	2006	dark brown

★ **MAXIMUM STITCH COUNT**
46 high x 51 wide

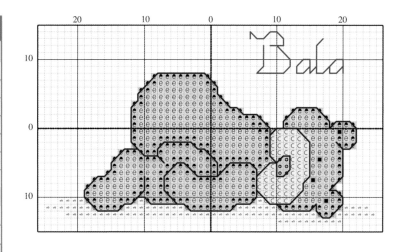

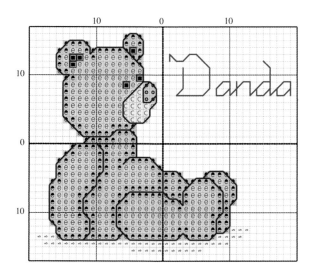

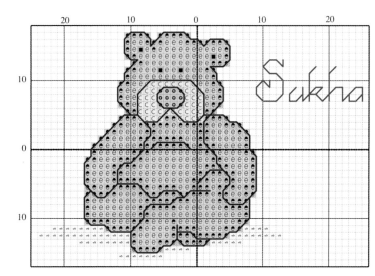

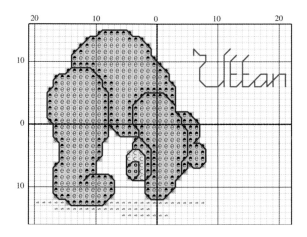

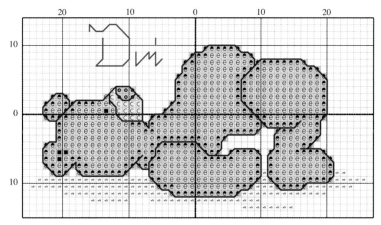

Be a Sport!

Use these charts to add a sporty feel. Work them on greeting cards, on a sports towel or a shoe bag – they would be an ideal choice for any budding sports man or woman! Choose from, on the opposite page, clockwise from top left, tennis, parachuting, football, car racing, diving and golf. On this page, clockwise from top left, you have fishing, karate and cricket

SPORTING TEDS KEY

★ **Cross stitch in two strands**

	DMC	Anchor	Madeira	
·	blanc	2	2402	white
■	310	403	2400	black
♥	349	13	0212	red
◖	414	235	1714	grey
◡	415	398	1802	light grey
▼	435	1046	2010	brown
▽	436	1045	2011	light brown
☆	518	1039	1106	blue
t	676	891	2208	sand
e	729	890	2209	dark sand
$	907	255	1308	green
⋄	973	290	0105	yellow

★ **Backstitch in one strand**

——	3799	236	1713	dark grey

★ **MAXIMUM STITCH COUNT**
40 high x 37 wide

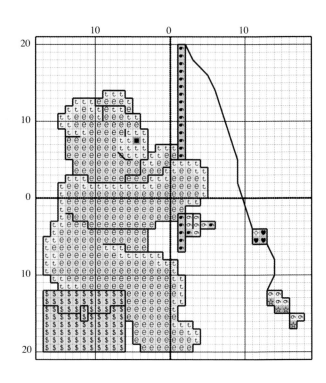

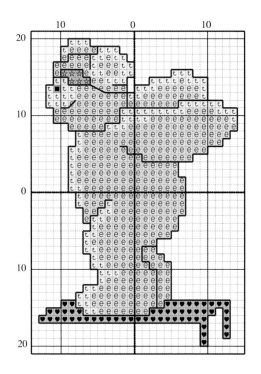

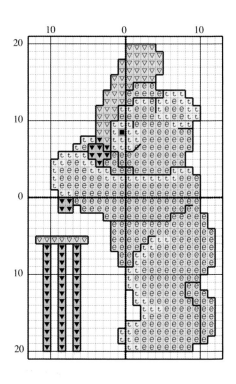

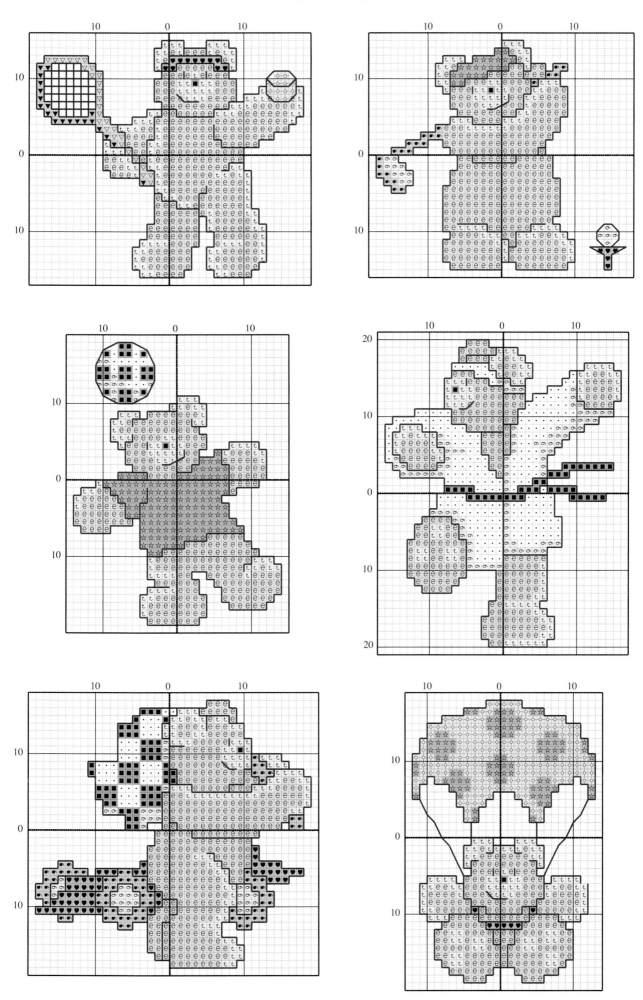

Fun in the Garden

*Use these quick and easy-to-work designs to decorate all sorts
of items around your home and surround yourself with teddies –
they've all got a gardening and garden fun theme to them. On these
and the next eight pages there are masses of little designs to choose
from – use them on book marks, key rings, greeting cards, note
books and little bags, or frame them as mini-pictures*

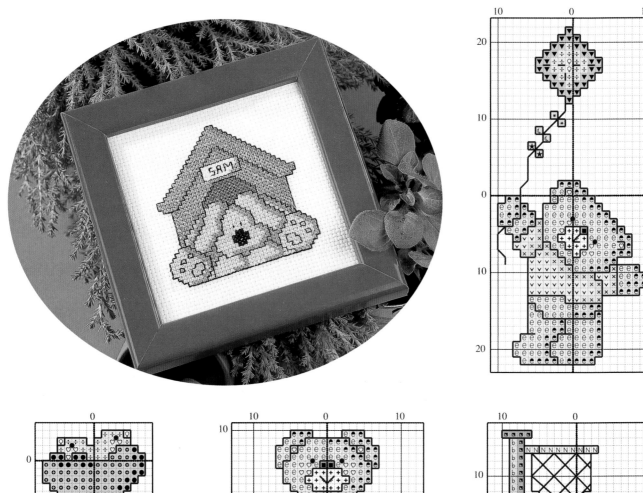

IN THE GARDEN KEY

★ **Cross stitch in two strands**

	DMC	Anchor	Madeira	
·	blanc	2	2402	white
♀	307	289	0104	lemon
■	310	403	2400	black
✹	317	400	1714	dark grey
$	318	399	1802	grey
◪	319	1044	1313	dark green
☾	340	118	0902	mauve
◥	367	217	1312	green
◿	368	214	1310	light green
◇	402	1047	2307	light ginger
N	415	398	1801	light grey
●	433	358	2602	dark brown
✿	435	1046	2010	brown
e	436	1045	2011	light brown
◦	444	291	0106	dark lemon
*	606	334	0209	bright orange
▼	701	227	1305	leaf green
▽	703	238	1307	lt leaf green
+	712	926	2101	cream
t	726	295	0109	yellow
e	738	367	2013	light tan
◩	798	137	0912	dark blue
b	799	145	0910	blue
∽	800	144	0908	sky blue
÷	809	130	0909	light blue
♥	817	13	0210	dark red
×	913	204	1212	mint green
v	955	206	1210	lt mint green
♡	957	50	0504	pink
★	970	925	0205	orange
☆	972	298	0107	dark yellow
☾	3746	1030	2702	purple
♦	3776	1048	2306	ginger

★ **Backstitch in one strand**

——	310	403	2400	black

★ **French knots in one strand**

●	310	403	2400	black

★ **MAXIMUM STITCH COUNT**
   44 high x 86 wide

The key for all the charts here and over the next eight pages.

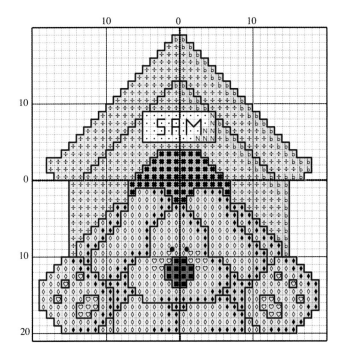

Above: *Make the dog sleeping in his kennel into the cutest of mini-pictures.*

Below: *Use the jolly ted with his bright balloons on a greeting card.*

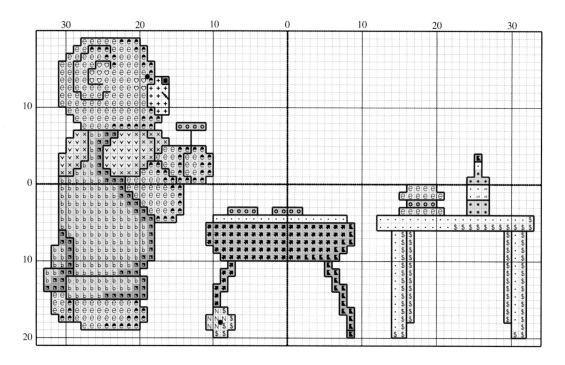

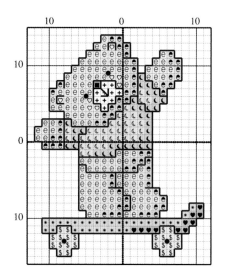

Pop a perky skate boarding bear into the front of a handy note book

*Use the picnic bears to make
a jolly book mark – ideal for
keeping your page in
that seed catalogue!*

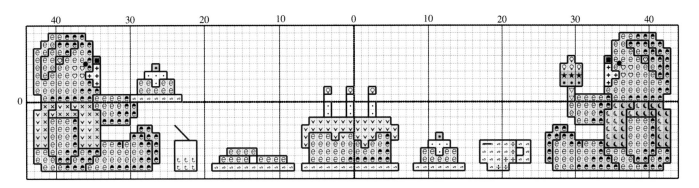

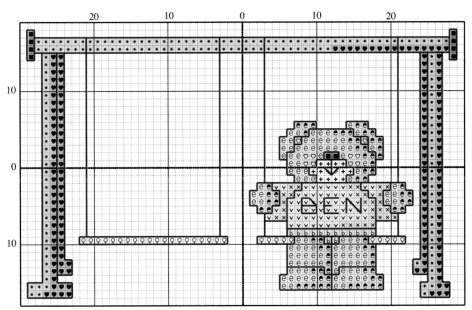

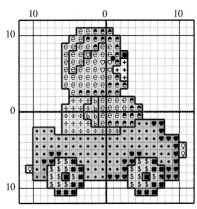

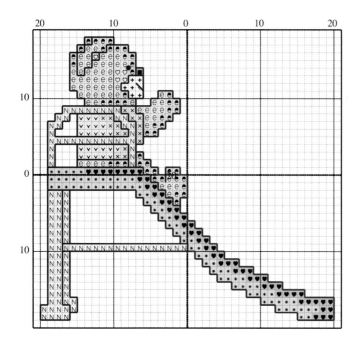

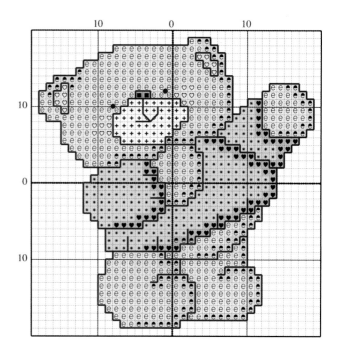

Slip a sliding bear onto the
front of a shoe bag – ideal for
either your play pumps or
your gardening shoes!

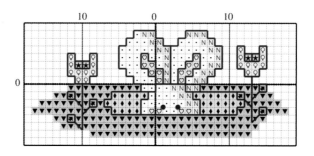

Sing out the praises of your gardening love with this little mini-picture.

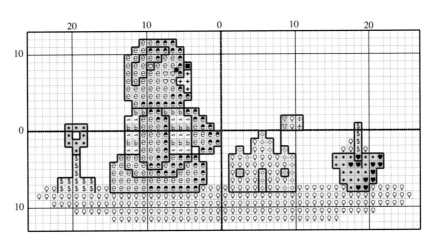

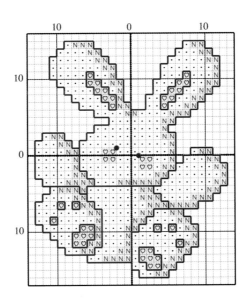

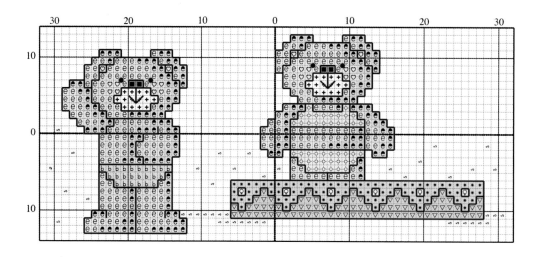

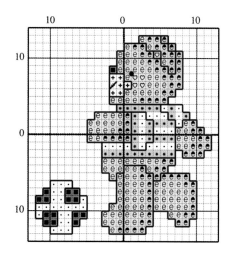

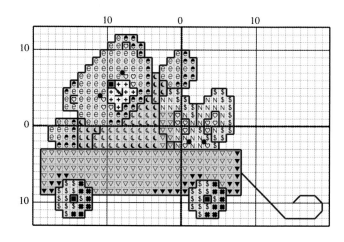

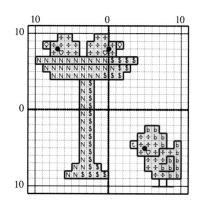

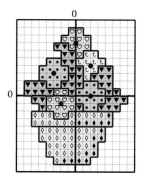

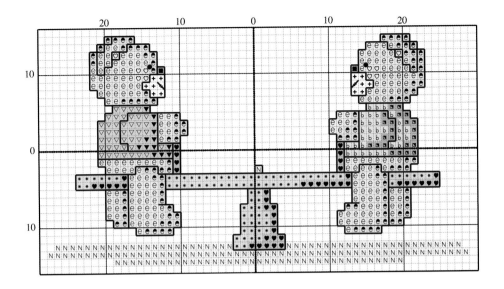

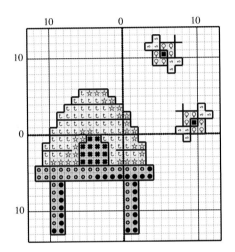

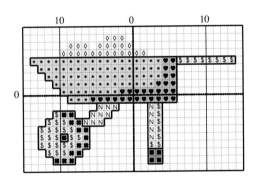

Pop a pretty pot of flowers into a key ring - ideal for the potting shed keys!

Make this mini-picture full of cooing doves in their home.

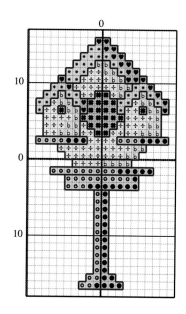

Make this greeting card to give with love - and a potted plant.

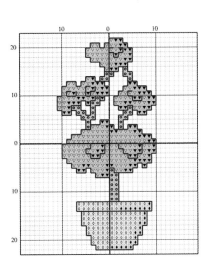

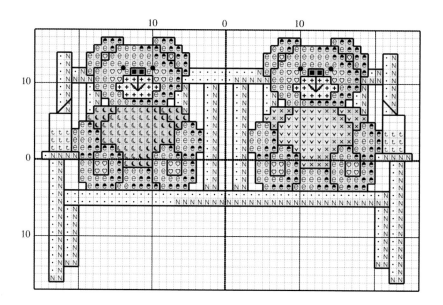

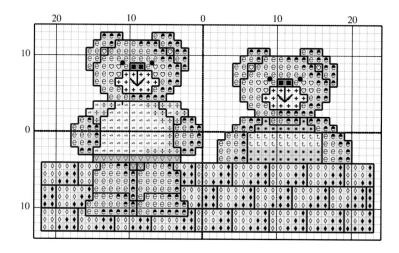

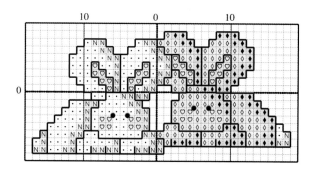

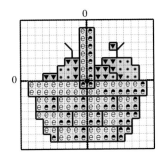
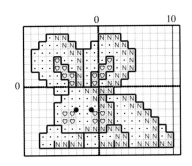
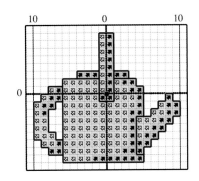

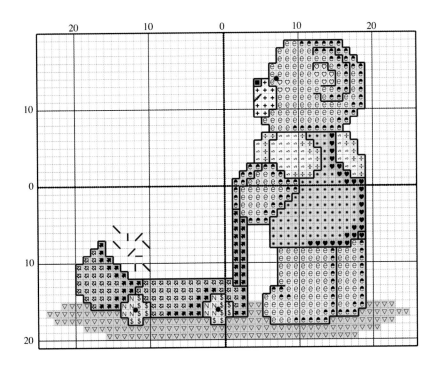

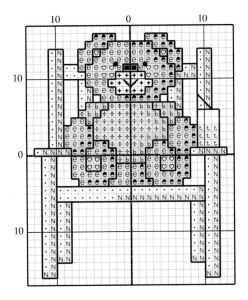

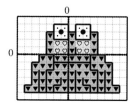

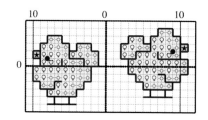

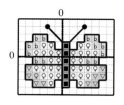

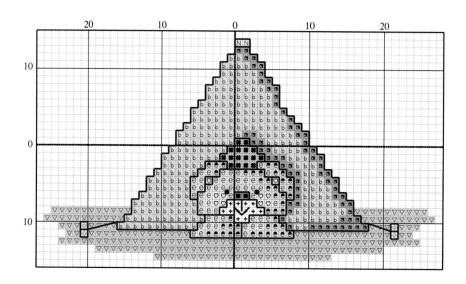

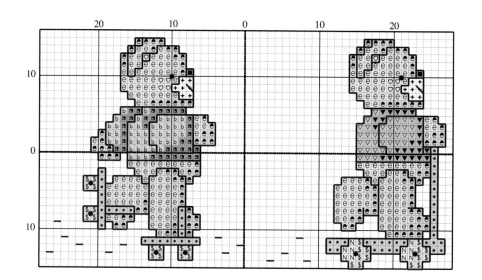